Easter Is Coming!

LENTEN CELEBRATIONS FOR THE FAMILY

by Mary and Herb Montgomery

WINSTON PRESS

ACKNOWLEDGEMENTS

Cover photo: Robert Friedman

Passages marked GN:
From the *Good News Bible*—Old Testament: copyright © American Bible Society 1976; New Testament: copyright © American Bible Society 1966, 1971, 1976.

Passages marked JB:
From *The Jerusalem Bible*, copyright © 1966 by Darton, Longman & Todd, Ltd. and Doubleday & Company, Inc. Used by permission of the publisher.

Passages marked KJV:
From the *King James Version*.

Passages marked NAB:
Scripture texts are taken from the *New American Bible*, copyright © 1970 by the Confraternity of Christian Doctrine, Washington, D.C. Used by permission of the copyright owner. All rights reserved.

Passages marked RSV:
Scripture quotations in this publication are from the *Revised Standard Version Common Bible*, copyright © 1973 by the Division of Christian Education of the National Council of the Churches of Christ in the U.S.A. Used by permission.

Library of Congress Catalog Card Number: 81-52024
ISBN: 0-86683-609-8
Printed in the United States of America

5   4   3   2

Winston Press, Inc.
430 Oak Grove
Minneapolis, Minnesota 55403

CONTENTS

PREFACE

A JOURNEY OF LOVE

When our children were little and seemed to need constant attention, we wondered if they'd ever grow up. Now they are nearly on their own and we wonder how their childhood years could have passed so swiftly! Our daughter is in college and our sons in high school, but the signs of their younger years are still everywhere in the house.

Hanging in a storage closet are three Easter baskets. When our children were little, the treat-filled baskets they discovered on Easter morning brought whoops of delight. Of course they understood nothing about the Resurrection in those early years, but they did associate Easter with the joy of discovery.

While preparing this book, we became aware of the many similarities between a family's life story and the lenten story. Our life, like Lent, involves a journey. Along the way there are great expectations, hope, death, and resurrection.

How hope-filled we are when we anticipate the birth of a child! How sad when a relative dies or when some important part of our life ends! And what of resurrection? There is surely a glimmer of this new life when a family is reconciled. What joy we feel when a friendship is mended or a personal problem is overcome! Lent is a time to look at the resurrections in our own lives. It is a time to dedicate ourselves to nurturing the love that makes them happen.

Family life is meant to be a journey of love, and that's what this book is about. In life there are always bumps and detours, but God seems to have created us in such a way that the problems of raising a family are eventually outweighed by the pleasures. Love makes the difference. In time, anger, jealousies, and disappointments tend to fade.

Perhaps you're a young parent just beginning your family journey and feeling a little unsure about how to observe Lent. Maybe you're well on your way to a grown-up family but have never done more than think about what you could or should do to observe the season. Whatever your situation, you'll find something useful in *Easter Is Coming!* It's a book for families large or small, those that include both a mom and dad and those with a single parent. We are all on a faith journey on which Jesus called us to "love one another."

Some of us are good at giving love but not at receiving it. Others are good at receiving love but never think to give it. If you have any difficulty with loving, Lent is a time for recognizing the need to change and taking steps to do so.

Traditionally Lent is a time to renew or rediscover the person God intends us to be. This involves us in prayer and serving others, fasting and worship. These activities develop our sense of the sacred and get us back in touch with our spiritual roots.

The Christian faith is one of hope because Jesus died and rose again. His love for us makes our salvation possible.

What we choose to do during the lenten season can give hope to others—to children, spouse, parents, friends, and even strangers whose lives we touch. May this book help you and your family feel the presence of the Lord as you make your preparation for Easter a journey of love.

INTRODUCTION

WAYS TO USE THIS BOOK

AS A FAMILY

Easter Is Coming! is a book of family devotions that covers every day of Lent. Each weekday there is a story from the life of Jesus and a prayer. There are ideas to share based on the readings, and activities to do both individually and as a family.

The stories about Jesus follow his life from birth through death and resurrection. They are adapted to be understood by children. If, however, you prefer to read the stories directly from Scripture, biblical references accompany each one.

The Ash Wednesday and Sunday devotions differ somewhat from those for weekdays. Ash Wednesday introduces the lenten theme of renewal. The Sunday devotions have as their theme "The Journey of Love." On this journey—which is developed through prayer, reading of Scripture, discussion, song, and family activities—we see possibilities for putting love into action in all aspects of our lives. With love in our lives, we travel the road of peace and fulfillment; we journey with God.

Certainly there are benefits to be had from family devotions, but how do we work them into an already-busy life? Usually we do it by settling for less than the ideal. It would, for instance, be ideal if the family could meet for devotions every day during Lent. Such a practice brings spiritual benefits known only to those who try it. But there are times—and they may be frequent—when conflicting schedules make it impossible for the entire family to get together. We suggest that at such times you proceed with those members who are available. Adults who are absent can read the materials at another time. Older children, too, can read the missed devotion, and younger ones might be read to or filled in by another family member. We'd like those who are absent not to feel guilty, but rather to feel that they've missed a positive family experience.

Often families who cannot commit their time regularly on weekdays are able to gather on Sundays. The time needed for the devotions is extremely flexible. The Scripture reading, sharing, and prayer can take as little as ten minutes—maybe even five at breakfast time! But depending upon the follow-up activity chosen, you can be involved for up to an hour or more. Whatever time you spend, you'll find it an excellent investment in togetherness where spiritual growth is possible for both individuals and the family.

Of course each family brings its own special talents to devotions. The ability to sing or play a musical instrument may be the key to your family's success. Perhaps someone has a dramatic reading voice or a skill at leading discussion. Make use of these talents, but also remember to give everyone a chance to make a contribution. Young and shy ones especially need the love and encouragement you can supply during your time together.

Following are suggestions for using the book:

1. Set a specific time for your devotions and proceed with those members who are available. Maybe you will decide to hold them at breakfast, after your evening meal, or at bedtime.
2. Read the story about Jesus aloud. Take turns with the readings, especially the stories. These are written simply so that children in the upper elementary grades will be able to read them with ease. Children whose reading skills are still developing can practice reading the story alone before reading it aloud to the family. This is a good time to encourage reading.
3. Share ideas that grow out of the story and the suggested questions. Much personal insight—and understanding of one another—can grow out of such sharing.
4. Pray together, adding petitions and intentions of your own.
5. Whenever possible, follow up with at least one of the activities suggested.

AS AN INDIVIDUAL

In paging through the book, you may notice that the right-hand pages for the weekday devotions seem to stand alone. The book has been designed that way for those family members who want something to turn to privately. The line from Scripture, the photograph, and the prayer work together to give a spiritual lift to your day.

If you find you're the family's "spiritual director" and not having much luck getting the family together for devotions, there are ways you can put this right-hand page to use. You might tear it out and put it on the refrigerator door. Add a new page each day and you'll soon have your family's attention. If there is a page that has particular relevance for one family member, you might take it out and tuck it in that person's notebook or lunch. Or you may find that a certain page would be perfect to send to a friend whose spirits need lifting. (Be sure, however, that you don't tear out a page until you have no further use for the materials on the other side.)

AS A TEACHER

Although *Easter Is Coming!* is intended for family use at home, it has applications in the classroom as well. The stories in the book are an excellent lenten review of the life of Jesus. Depending upon the grade you teach, the stories can either be read to the children or by the children themselves. If you're working in the upper grades, the pages with the photographs can be put on the bulletin board. Some of the prayers make good discussion-starters about individual responsibility for helping make home a place of contentment and harmony.

SYMBOLS OF LENT

Our Christian tradition is rich in symbols. To name but a few, we have the star, symbolizing Christ's birth; the cross, symbolizing his life, death and resurrection; the fish, symbolizing the early Christians' faith in Jesus. During Lent, we use symbols that relate to the themes of the season—the themes of repentance, renewal, hope, and joy. Following are some of our Lenten symbols:

Ashes symbolize death and grief as well as the unworthiness and repentance we feel because we have not lived up to being the person God intends us to be. But out of the ashes of our past we can, with God's help, be renewed spiritually and journey to a new life of faith and trust. Ash Wednesday marks the beginning of our journey.

Colors are symbolic. Violet signifies suffering and sorrow; white, purity and glory; green, growth and hope of eternal life; pink or rose, joy.

A *bare branch* symbolizes Jesus' death on a wooden cross. It also reminds us that out of seeming lifelessness comes new life, both in nature and in the Resurrection.

The butterfly dramatically symbolizes new life and is commonly used to help children begin to understand the meaning of Easter. Out of a dead-looking cocoon emerges a new creation, free and radiant.

Salt is necessary to sustain life and is a symbol of wholeness. We use salt as a preservative to keep food wholesome. We also use it as a flavoring that permeates the whole of whatever it is added to.

Water has always been a symbol of cleansing and life-giving in the Church and is commonly associated with Baptism. In Scripture, Jesus speaks of himself as the "life-giving water" (John 4:14), the one who quenches our spiritual thirst.

Light is a universal religious symbol which reminds us that Jesus is the light who shows us the way. "I am the light of the world" (John 9:5), Jesus tells us. "He who follows me will not walk in darkness, but will have the light of life" (John 8:12).

Seeds symbolize the emergence of new life. Seemingly lifeless seeds grow and flower. Like the emerging butterfly, the emerging plant symbolizes the new life that follows Christ's death and Resurrection.

Palm branches symbolize Jesus' triumphal entry into Jerusalem the Sunday before his crucifixion. The branches remind us that there are both triumphs and defeats in our lives but that if we maintain our friendship with God, we will ultimately triumph.

The Easter lily, with its waxy flowers shaped like trumpets, symbolizes the glory of the risen Lord and the joy of the faithful who believe in God's promise of new life.

Young children do not understand the meaning of symbols. They do, however, value what we value. Our attitude toward the use of symbols at home and in church prepares children to seek a deeper meaning as they grow older.

FASTING

Each year as Lent approaches, our own children begin discussing what food they're going to "give up." After joking about foregoing foods as out-of-season as peaches and blueberries, they settle on some treat they enjoy and will miss. Maybe it's candy or pop or ice cream. Once they've made their commitments, they of course want to know what their parents are denying themselves!

Fasting is in keeping with the penitential character of the season. It has its roots deep in the history of God's people. In the Hebrew Scriptures (Old Testament), annual fasts mark disasters in Jewish history. Generally their fasts meant going without all food or drink. There are also accounts of occasional fasts by individuals and groups. These gave expression to grief or penitence or were thought to be useful in securing God's help. The Christian Scriptures (New Testament) reveal Jesus fasting in the wilderness, and we see a belief in the value of fasting persisting in the early Church.

What is the value of fasting in contemporary life? Does the "giving up" of food or drink during Lent serve any worthwhile purpose? If we think of fasting as a negative action, probably not. But if we see the time of fasting as an opportunity to think and act positively, the experience can be spiritually enriching.

We've found that when we and our children deny ourselves something, however small, it's a constant reminder that we are in the lenten season and have made a choice to live in a particular way. Fasting gives us a perspective on what is necessary and what is excessive. By cutting back on food we realize that we normally consume more than we need. This may lead to the realization that we might simplify our lives in other ways as well.

Even though adults and older children make commitments to fast on their own, it's doubly enriching to fast as a family. While the family fasts, there's a "we're-in-this-together" spirit that adds a special quality to the lenten experience. When deciding how the family will fast, include everyone. People of all ages are more inclined to be cooperative about a plan they helped make than one that is imposed on them. Whatever you decide to do should be reasonable for your family. Take into

account the ages of your children. Those in preschool and the early grades need understanding and support in curbing their desires for food. If fasting is too rigorous, it's likely to be abandoned after the initial enthusiasm wears off, and the purpose is then defeated. Following are some fasting possibilities for the family:

—Do away with snacks between meals.
—Eliminate junk foods such as potato chips, pop, and sugary treats.
—Eliminate desserts.
—Once or twice a week, serve a simple meal that consists of soup or salad, bread, and a beverage.
—Serve meat half as often as usual.
—Abide by any fasting regulations of your church.

Consider giving whatever money you save by your fasting to help the needy of the world. Possibly, you can make a donation to a home for battered women and children in your community or to some local food-distribution service. Or you may choose to take part in a project such as Operation Rice Bowl through your church. This program, designed to help feed the hungry both here and around the world, asks that you eat a simple soup or salad meal one day a week and put the money you save on food into a cardboard rice bowl provided for participants. When the bowl is left on the kitchen table, children see that their fasting provides money which will benefit someone less fortunate. Children have even been known to dip into their own pockets and piggy banks to make donations. Fasting, concern for our neighbors, and almsgiving are ways to renew ourselves in mind and spirit during Lent.

SELF-EXAMINATION

Lent is a time to "get right" with the Lord and everyone else we know. Most of us recognize our personal weaknesses all too well. But we tend to gloss over them, hiding or ignoring faults that tarnish the good stuff we're made of. Remember, we're created in the image of God—but God has given us the freedom to choose. And we've *all* made some sinful choices. The wonderful thing about Easter is that it's a perfect time to die to an old way of living and begin anew, a perfect time to ask ourselves, "How's my relationship with myself? My spouse? My parents? My children? My brothers and sisters? My boss? My God?"

A newspaper reported a story about a letter and some cash received by a department store. Someone had returned payment for merchandise stolen twenty years before. Imagine the feeling of being free of guilt after all those years!

In another story, a busy executive whose son was on drugs saw the youth successfully rehabilitated. The father had never been able to express his emotions, but with help was finally able to face his son and say, "I love you." A short while later, the son was killed while being robbed at the store where he worked. Despite the father's grief, imagine how grateful he was for having expressed his real feelings while he had the chance.

Is there someone you need to repay? Someone you should forgive? Someone to whom you could give more time and love?

This Lent, take time alone. Examine those things you've hidden or glossed over in your life. Then take the necessary steps to get right with yourself, your spouse, your children, your boss. You'll find that in doing so you're also getting right with God. Repentance and confession will lead you in a new direction. The change will fill you with new life. And that's what Easter is all about!

RECIPES

HOT CROSS BUNS

2 packages active dry yeast
1/3 cup water
1/3 cup milk, scalded
1/2 cup salad oil or melted shortening
1/3 cup sugar
3/4 tsp. salt
3½ to 4 cups sifted flour
1/2 to 1 tsp. cinnamon
3 eggs
2/3 cup currants or raisins
1 slightly beaten egg white
sifted confectioner's sugar

Soften yeast in warm water. Combine milk, salad oil, sugar, and salt; cool to lukewarm. Sift together 1 cup flour and cinnamon; stir into milk mixture. Add eggs; beat well. Stir in yeast and currants or raisins. Add remaining flour to make a soft dough. Cover with a damp cloth. Let rise in warm place until double (about 1½ hours). Punch down. Roll or pat out to ½-inch thickness on lightly floured surface. Cut in rounds with 2½-inch biscuit cutter. Place on greased baking sheet about 1½ inches apart. Cover and let rise until almost double (about 1 hour). Cut shallow cross in each bun with scissors. Brush tops with egg white. Bake in moderate oven (350° or 375°) 12 to 15 minutes or until done. Add confectioner's sugar to remaining egg white. Use this as a frosting for piping on warm buns. Makes about 2 dozen.

PASSOVER SALAD

The sweet taste is a reminder of the slavery that is now ended.

6 medium apples, grated or chopped fine
1/2 cup raisins
1/2 cup chopped nuts
1 tsp. cinnamon
1/4 cup wine

Mix and serve.

PRETZEL RECIPE

1 pkg. yeast
1¼ cup warm water
1 tsp. salt
1 tbsp. sugar
1/4 cup melted margarine or butter
1/4 cup wheat germ
3¾ cups flour
1 egg
coarse salt

Dissolve yeast in water. Add the next five ingredients in the order given. Knead the dough until smooth, adding flour as necessary. Roll the dough between hands to form long, pencil-thin rope. Put lightly beaten egg in a shallow bowl. In another bowl, put coarse salt. Take 8-inch lengths of dough. Holding the ends, dip one side of the lengths first into the egg and then lightly into the salt. Place on a heavily greased cookie sheet with the salt side up. Bend into "little arms," crosses, and other shapes symbolic of Lent. Bake at 425° until well browned.

SONGS

JESUS CHRIST IS RISEN TODAY

Latin hymn

Lyra Davidica

1. Je - sus Christ is risen to - day, Al - - le - lu - ia!
2. Hymns of praise then let us sing, Al - - le - lu - ia!
3. But the pains which he en - dured, Al - - le - lu - ia!

1. Our tri - um - phant ho - ly day, Al - - le - lu - ia!
2. Un - to Christ, our heaven - ly King, Al - - le - lu - ia!
3. Our sal - va - tion have pro - cured, Al - - le - lu - ia!

1. Who did once up - on the cross, Al - - le - lu - ia!
2. Who en - dured the cross and grave, Al - - le - lu - ia!
3. Now he rules, e - ter - nal King, Al - - le - lu - ia!

1. Suf - fer to re - deem our loss, Al - - le - lu - ia! 2.
2. Sin - ners to re - deem and save, Al - - le - lu - ia! 3.
3. Where the an - gels ev - er sing, Al - - le - lu - ia!

THIS LITTLE LIGHT OF MINE

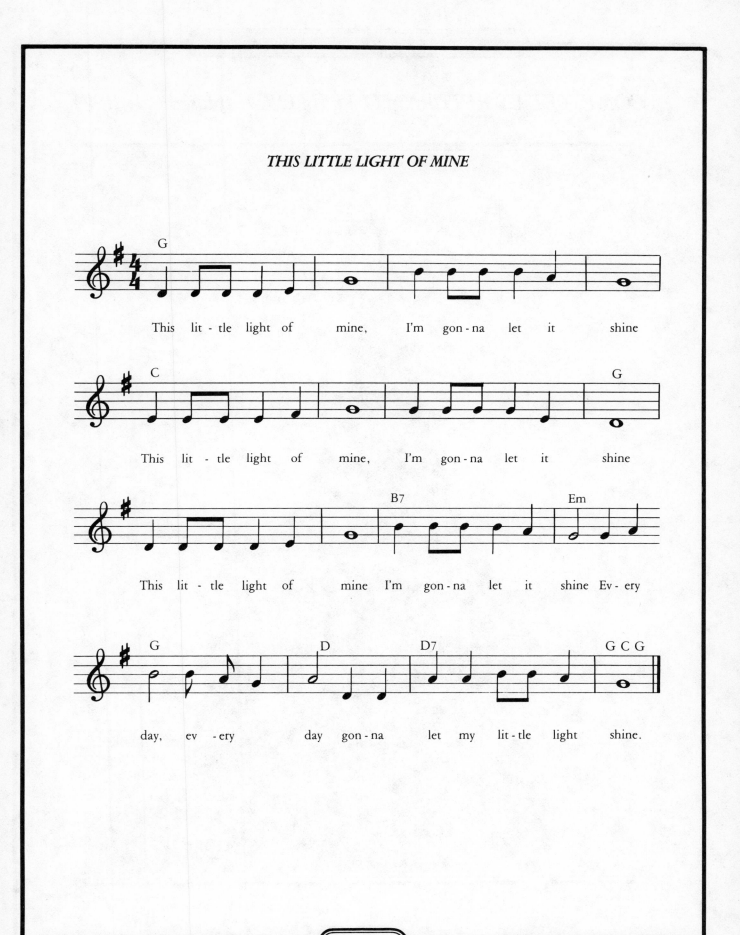

This lit - tle light of mine, I'm gon - na let it shine

This lit - tle light of mine, I'm gon - na let it shine

This lit - tle light of mine I'm gon - na let it shine Ev - ery

day, ev - ery day gon - na let my lit - tle light shine.

COME, LET US RETURN TO THE LORD. *(Hosea 6:1, RSV)*

GATHER

Gather the family around a table or wherever you can all be comfortable and have eye contact with one another. Be close enough that you can easily join hands while praying. Establish a relaxed and informal atmosphere, one which suggests that your lenten devotions are going to be enjoyable, positive experiences to which everyone may contribute. Explain why you're gathering and what your hopes for the family are this lenten season.

Since it is up to the leader to get things going and guide discussion, choose an adult or teen to act as leader the first few times you gather. Also choose two readers. As everyone becomes more familiar with the devotions, take turns serving as leader and readers. (Be sure that everyone who wants to lead or read has a turn sometime during Lent.)

LIGHT A CANDLE

Begin by lighting a special candle, one set aside for use only during your family devotions. Purchase a large, decorative candle, or create your own Easter—Paschal—candle. Place a large candle in a shallow glass dish. Stick five cloves in the candle to form a cross. Flowers or greenery can be floated at the base of the candle as a symbol of new life. Invite family members to take turns lighting the candle. With supervision, even young children can have a turn.

SING

The song "This Little Light of Mine" on page 11 is suggested as the theme song for today and for all the Sundays during Lent. It's an easy song for young children to learn and sing, and reminds us that Jesus is the light of the world. In turn, we are called to be a light to others. (Of course you may sing any song your family considers appropriate. Or if you're a nonsinging family, play a recorded hymn.)

PRAY

Leader: Let's join hands as we pray.

Dear Lord, we gather in your name on this Ash Wednesday. We thank you for all the blessings we have received. And we ask your help in making our family devotions a time of growing closer to one another and to you. Amen.

READ SCRIPTURE

First Reader: The apostle Paul was one of the greatest preachers and organizers in the early church. Today's reading is from his letter to the Romans.

God puts people right through their faith in Jesus Christ. God does this to all who believe in Christ, because there is no difference at all: everyone has sinned and is far away from God's saving presence. But by the free gift of God's grace all are put right with him through Christ Jesus, who sets them free.

Romans 3:22-24, GN

SHARE AND REFLECT

Second Reader: Lent is a time to look at our lives and think about the way we have been living. There is much in our life that is good. But we also know that we do things that hurt one another and are displeasing to God. During Lent, we can build on what is good in our family. And we can change those things that prevent us from being the loving people God would like us to be. Let's recall some of the good things about belonging to our family.

How is our family special?

What would we like to change about the way our family lives? Is there something we could change during Lent?

What have we done to observe Lent in years past? What are we going to do this year? Will we fast? Have a schedule for family devotions? Attend lenten services at our church?

CLOSE WITH A PRAYER

Leader: Lord, we thank you for our family and the times we have together. Help us to be aware of the ways in which we can change and grow to become more loving people. Open our eyes to the ways we can "get right" with you and everyone we know. Amen.

FOLLOW UP

Extend your family time together by doing one or more of the following activities during the coming week.

Ashes are the symbol used at the beginning of Lent to remind us that all things die but that as Christians we believe that we will have new life. Bless family members and mark their foreheads with a cross drawn with ashes. (Ashes can be obtained by burning palm fronds saved from last year. Or use soot which you get by holding a spoon close over the candle flame—just be careful you don't burn your fingers.)

Make a wooden cross by tying two sticks or nailing two narrow boards together. Set the cross in a container filled with sand and use it in family devotions. Add a growing vine to the base of the cross as a reminder of new life.

Plant an amaryllis bulb. Planted now, it will bloom close to Easter.

TREATS

Normally at this time in your Sunday devotions you'll share a treat. Today, however, fast to mark Ash Wednesday and the beginning of this penitential season.

AN ANGEL VISITS MARY

For many years, the Israelites had waited for God to send them a savior. Jesus was to fulfill that role. The life of Jesus begins with the story of an angel coming to a young woman named Mary. In our story for today, we hear about that visit. (Luke 1:26-38)

God sent the angel Gabriel to a city in Galilee called Nazareth. There the angel appeared to Mary, who was engaged to a man named Joseph. The angel said, "Hail, favored one. The Lord is with you."

Mary was surprised and greatly troubled by the angel's words. What sort of greeting was this?

The angel said, "Do not be afraid, Mary. God is very pleased with you. You are going to have a son and you will name him Jesus. He will be great and will be called the Son of the Most High. There will be no end to his kingdom."

Still, Mary was troubled. "How can this be?" she asked. "I have no husband."

The angel said to her, "The Holy Spirit will come upon you and the power of God will be with you. The child to be born will be called the Son of God."

The angel had still more news for Mary. "Your cousin Elizabeth is also going to have a baby even though she is thought to be too old. But with God, nothing is impossible."

Mary said, "I am the handmaid of the Lord; I will do whatever God asks of me."

SHARE

Many of the people we read about in the Bible appear to know clearly what God intends for them. Certainly Mary's call was evident. But what about those of us who walk the earth today? God's calls to us are usually not so attention-getting as being visited by an angel. Instead God is more likely to speak to us through a friend, through a persistent inner urging, through the Scriptures. Do we listen for God's call? Lent is a good time to listen and to share our dreams and aspirations with others. What hopes do each of us have?

FOLLOW UP

Much of what we are exposed to through newspapers, news magazines, radio and TV news programs gives the impression that violence and evil are winning out over peace and love. Brainstorm for ways to build a good family life. Make a list. (For example: Hug Mom. Hug Dad. Help out. Apologize for hurts. Watch and discuss a TV program.) Then cut out 44 strips (1" x 6") of plain paper. Print one family-building idea per strip. (Ideas can be used more than once.) Make a chain by pasting or taping the strips together to form links. Fasten the chain to a cross and remove one link per day as you count down to Easter.

ENCOURAGE ONE ANOTHER AND BUILD ONE ANOTHER UP. (1 Thessalonians 5:11, RSV)

Lord, you have given us life.
You have created us for a purpose.
But discovering that purpose is not always easy.
There are times when we feel lost and alone,
times when we see no meaning and have no goal.
In our confusion and indecision,
may we never stop trusting you, Lord.
Help us to know that you always hear our prayers
and will guide us in the way we should go. Amen.

MARY VISITS ELIZABETH

When Mary heard that her cousin Elizabeth was also going to have a baby, she set out alone to visit her. In our story for today, we hear about their meeting. (Luke 1:39-49)

Mary went quickly into the hill country to the town where Elizabeth lived. As Mary entered her cousin's house, she called out a greeting.

When Elizabeth heard her cousin's call, she was filled with the Holy Spirit. She cried out to Mary, "Blessed are you among women and blessed is the baby you will have." Then she said, "Why am I so honored as to be visited by the mother of our Lord? The baby within me leaped for joy when you called out your greeting. You are blessed to believe what the Lord has spoken to you."

Mary said to Elizabeth:
"My soul magnifies the Lord
and my spirit rejoices in God my Savior,
for he has regarded the low estate of his handmaiden.
For behold, henceforth all generations will call me blessed;
for he who is mighty has done great things for me,
and holy is his name. . . ."

SHARE

Mary's rush to share her exciting news with Elizabeth may remind us of times when we've had good news and wanted to let others know about it. Let's recall some of the good news from our recent past. What good news have we had at work? At school? At home? With whom do we like to share such news? How good are we at listening to what others want to share?

FOLLOW UP

Most of us are quick to complain when we feel we've been unjustly treated. But we're not so prone to compliment those who have in some way made our life better. Look for ways to share the love which God has so generously given. Send a note of appreciation to a thoughtful boss, an understanding teacher, a coach, the mayor, or a librarian.

Begin a bulletin board of good news. Watch the papers for stories that reveal people's concern for one another.

Share the feelings of excitement experienced by each family member when a baby was on the way.

YOU WILL SHOW ME THE PATH TO LIFE.
(Psalm 16:11, NAB)

We know there is a path that leads to you, Lord.
But often we turn away
and head in the direction of our own self interests.
Whenever that happens, we lose sight of our goal.
Lord, we admit our need for your constant, loving guidance.
Make us ever aware of what it is you want us to do.
Then fill us with the courage and purpose we need
to head in that direction. Amen.

JESUS IS BORN

At about the time Mary was to give birth, Caesar Augustus ordered that a census be taken. This meant that Mary and Joseph had to go to Bethlehem, a long journey over difficult roads. When they reached Bethlehem, they found the city overflowing with people. In our story for today, we hear what happened then. (Luke 2:1-14)

While Mary and Joseph were in Bethlehem, the time came for Mary to have her baby. But there was no room for them at any of the inns. So she and Joseph found shelter in a place used to protect animals from the wind and cold. There Mary gave birth. She wrapped Jesus in linen cloths and laid him in a manger.

Nearby, there were shepherds keeping watch over their flocks by night. An angel appeared to them and the glory of the Lord shone round about. The shepherds were frightened, but the angel said to them, "Do not be afraid, for I bring you good news of great joy. In the city of David, a Savior who is Christ the Lord has been born today. And this will be a sign to you: you will find a baby wrapped in swaddling clothes and lying in a manger."

Suddenly there were many angels praising God and saying, "Glory to God in the highest, and on earth peace to those of good will."

SHARE

It's well past Christmas now, but hearing the Christmas story can remind us of the holiday season. During those busy days, we may have been so involved with preparations that the greatest gift of all was a bit overlooked. Let's review what has happened since our exchange of gifts at Christmas. Have any of our presents been broken? Lost? Forgotten? And what about God's gift to us? Have we broken away from Jesus, lost interest in him, or maybe even forgotten why God sent his Son?

FOLLOW UP

Lent is a time to "get right" with God, and that includes affirming the place Jesus has in our lives.

Forgive someone who has hurt you.

Donate the money you save by fasting to any group that feeds the hungry.

Invite neighbors to join your family for an evening of religious discussion and prayer.

GOD...LOVED US AND SENT HIS SON TO BE THE MEANS BY WHICH OUR SINS ARE FORGIVEN.
(1 John 4:10, GN)

Help us, Lord, to look upon the cross
as a sign that life will always include hope—
hope for the sick, the lonely, the old.
Whatever our situation,
we have reason to hope
because you sent your Son.
Jesus tells us of your love, your forgiveness,
your promise of life to come.
His coming makes all the difference.
Please help us remember that
each time we look upon the cross. Amen.

OPEN WIDE YOUR HAND TO YOUR BROTHER, TO THE NEEDY AND TO THE POOR, IN THE LAND.
(Deuteronomy 15:11, RSV)

GATHER

Gather the family around a table or wherever you can all be comfortable and have eye contact with one another. Be close enough so that you can easily join hands while praying. Establish a relaxed and informal atmosphere. Choose a leader and two readers.

LIGHT A CANDLE

Light a candle as a sign to everyone that the time you spend together has special significance — you are placing yourselves in the presence of the Lord.

SING

Sing "This Little Light of Mine" on page 11, the suggested theme song for all the Sundays during Lent. (Of course you may sing any song your family considers appropriate. Or if you're a non-singing family, play a recorded hymn.)

PRAY

Leader: Let's join hands as we pray.

Dear Lord, we gather in your name on this first Sunday in Lent. Thank you for giving us life and the opportunity to be together as a family. Please help us understand how important love is in our lives. Let us feel your presence today as we begin to make this lenten season a journey of love. Amen.

READ SCRIPTURE

First Reader: The apostle Paul wrote many letters to people who chose to become Christians. One of the people he wrote to was a man named Philemon. In one of his letters, Paul wrote:

Brother Philemon, every time I pray, I mention you and give thanks to my God. For I hear of your love for all of God's people and the faith you have in the Lord Jesus. My prayer is that our fellowship with you as believers will bring about a deeper understanding of every blessing which we have in our life in union with Christ. Your love, dear brother, has brought me great joy and much encouragement! You have cheered the hearts of all of God's people.

Philemon verses 4-7, GN

SHARE AND REFLECT

Second Reader: Paul was not always a Christian. In fact, before his conversion, he thought it was foolish for anyone to follow Christ. But Paul experienced a dramatic change of heart. Not only did he become a Christian but he also dedicated himself to spreading the good news. Paul's letter-writing to fellow Christians reminds us that we can use our hands to express the love we feel. Today we're going to talk about the "Hand of Love" and the many ways we use our hands to show concern and affection.

Let's look closely at our hands. Who has the largest hands? When are large hands especially useful? Who has the smallest hands? When are small hands especially useful?

How many ways can we think of to use our hands to express friendliness?

Helping one another is a way of expressing love. In a typical day, how do we use our hands to be helpful at home?

CLOSE WITH A PRAYER

Leader: Lord, help us this week to stretch out the "hand of love" to those we meet at work, at school, and at play. Remind us that the gentle touch of a hand can sometimes say more than words. Help us use our hands to heal instead of hurt, to build instead of break. Thank you for hands both large and small and for opportunities to use them in your service. Amen.

FOLLOW UP

Extend your family time together by doing one or more of the following activities.

On this journey toward Easter, make a special effort to be the hand of love in relationships with others. Begin by communicating love through letters. Write to a friend or relative who would enjoy hearing from your family. Compose a family letter, or have each member write individually. Young children can draw pictures to enclose.

Create a "Helping Hands" poster. Draw around each person's hands on a large sheet of paper. Then color in the outlines. (Or wet palms and fingers with poster paint and press on paper.) Display the work.

Make pretzels (see the recipe on page 9). Early Christians living in the Roman Empire made small breads of water, flour and salt and shaped them in the form of arms crossed in prayer. These were called *bracellae* or "little arms." From the Latin, the Germans coined the word *pretzel*.

TREATS

Serve the freshly baked pretzels.

THE FLIGHT TO EGYPT

Some wise men from the East followed a star to the place where Jesus lay. When Herod, the ruler, learned that important people were seeking out Jesus, he was greatly troubled. Would this child grow up and take away his throne? To avoid this possibility, Herod ordered that all baby boys in and around Bethlehem be killed. In our story for today, we learn how Jesus was spared. (Matthew 2:13-15, 19-23)

After the wise men left, an angel of the Lord appeared to Joseph in a dream. "Rise," the angel said, "take the child and his mother and flee to Egypt. Remain there until I tell you it is safe. Herod plans to search for the child and kill him."

During the night, Joseph fled with Mary and the child Jesus. They went to Egypt where they stayed until Herod died.

After Herod's death, an angel again appeared to Joseph. "Rise," the angel said, "take the child and his mother and return to the land of Israel. Those who wanted to kill the child are now dead."

Joseph took Jesus and Mary, and together they set off for Israel. But when Joseph heard that Herod's son was now the ruler in Israel, he went instead to the city of Nazareth in Galilee. There the family made its home.

SHARE

Mary and Joseph had to flee from their homeland to protect Jesus. A lot of people share similar experiences. Many people in the United States have fled from their homelands in Europe, Vietnam, Cambodia, Cuba, Mexico, Haiti. Officially, how does our country treat refugees? How do we ourselves feel about allowing refugees into our country? What stories about leaving a homeland does our family history include?

FOLLOW UP

The Europeans who came to the United States because of World War II were referred to as displaced persons. But there are many other ways to be displaced. The newly divorced, the unemployed, the abused, the mentally retarded, the physically handicapped—all are prone to feel that it's an uncaring world in which they have no secure place. Consider what you can do to help someone who feels abandoned and lonely.

Take in a foster child, if possible.

Befriend, or at least not put down, a "different" person who is in a special class at school.

Don't gossip.

Join a social action group sponsored by your church.

FEAR NOT FOR I AM WITH YOU. (Isaiah 43:5, RSV)

Lord, it's such a hurtful thing to be displaced,
to feel unwanted and unnecessary.
Everything that once seemed secure and certain
comes into question.
Why don't people fit in? Is it the color of their skin?
The clothes they wear? The way they look or speak?
Their religion? The work they do?
Please, Lord, let those who are displaced
feel your love.
Help those of us who might reveal your love
stretch out the hand of understanding and friendship. Amen.

JESUS IS PRESENTED IN THE TEMPLE

Jewish law required that Mary and Joseph present Jesus in the Temple forty days after his birth. Our story for today tells us about that event. (Luke 2:22-35, 39)

When it came time for Jesus to be presented in the Temple, Mary and Joseph brought him to Jerusalem. It happened that there was an old man living there whose name was Simeon. Simeon loved God and led a good life. The Holy Spirit had revealed to him that he would not die before he had seen the Son of God.

Inspired by the Spirit, Simeon went to the Temple on the very day that Mary and Joseph were presenting Jesus. When Simeon saw the baby Jesus, he took him in his arms and gave thanks to God.

"Lord," Simeon said, "your servant can now die in peace, for my eyes have seen the one you promised to send. Salvation has come and it will be for all people."

Mary and Joseph were amazed at Simeon's words. When they had done everything according to the law of the Lord, they left the Temple and took Jesus home with them.

SHARE

In bringing Jesus to the Temple, Mary and Joseph were fulfilling their parental duties. Parents have always had special responsibilities for the religious upbringing of their children. A time comes, however, when parents no longer have the main responsibility. Let's discuss how we feel about a parent's role in religious education. How does it differ at the time of confirmation from what it was at the time of baptism? Do we view participation in religious education classes and worship as an obligation, or as an opportunity? How does our viewpoint affect our relationship with God? Is our relationship one of love, or of fear? What religious attitudes are the adults in our family passing along to the children?

FOLLOW UP

No club or organization (including the church) operates successfully for long without a core of dedicated people, including leaders *and* followers.

At your church, volunteer to teach a class, join a committee, or take care of the younger children while the adults are meeting.

At home, dedicate yourself to making bedtime a time of peace and gentle love for the children in the family. Sing, read, pray, take time to listen.

Attend church as a family.

BE DOERS OF THE WORD, AND NOT HEARERS ONLY.
(James 1:22, RSV)

I am only one, Lord,
but I am one.
I cannot do everything,
but I can do something.
What I can do,
I ought to do.
And what I ought to do,
by your grace, I will do. Amen.

Prayer from The Christophers

JESUS STAYS BEHIND IN JERUSALEM

The Scriptures tell us very little about the childhood of Jesus. But in our story for today, we learn something that happened during his growing-up years. (Luke 2:41-52)

Every year at the feast of Passover, Mary and Joseph went to Jerusalem. When Jesus was twelve, they made the trip as they always had. But when the feast was over and they were returning home, Jesus was not with the caravan. It wasn't until evening that Mary and Joseph discovered he was missing. When they couldn't find him among their friends and neighbors, they became very worried and returned to Jerusalem. After three days of searching, Mary and Joseph found Jesus in the Temple. He was sitting among the teachers, listening to them and asking questions. All who heard him were amazed at his understanding and his answers.

Mary said to Jesus, "Son, why have you done this to us? Your father and I have been very worried about you."

Jesus replied, "Why did you come looking for me? Did you not know that I must be about my Father's business?"

Mary and Joseph did not understand Jesus' answer. But he left the Temple with them, and the three of them returned to Nazareth together.

SHARE

We might imagine that Mary and Joseph had mixed feelings about Jesus' behavior as he was growing up and doing more on his own. Of course parents want their children to become independent people who can care for themselves. But it sometimes seems that children want too much independence too soon. What growing-up experiences has our family already had? (Remember "firsts": first words, first steps, first school day.) As parents, how were we granted—or not granted—independence by our parents? As children, how are we granted—or not granted— independence by our parents?

FOLLOW UP

Cooperate as a family to set appropriate age-level guidelines for such things as allowances, bedtimes, household responsibilities. (With older children, work out guidelines about driving, hours, dating.)

Review your TV-watching habits. What show is your family not viewing that you might benefit from? (Consider news shows, documentaries, specials.)

ACCEPT INSTRUCTION, THAT YOU MAY GAIN IN WISDOM FOR THE FUTURE. (Proverbs 19:20, RSV)

Lord, there's something new to be learned every day,
but learning is not always easy.
It takes time to learn how to read
or play a musical instrument.
It takes patience to learn how to ride a bike
or operate a computer.
When we don't learn as quickly as we'd like,
we become discouraged.
Be with us, Lord, as we grow in knowledge
and try new skills.
Help us realize that making mistakes is part of learning.
Grant us the understanding that we fail
only when we refuse to try again. Amen.

JOHN THE BAPTIZER PREPARES THE WAY

Before Jesus began his ministry of teaching and healing, his cousin John prepared the way. In our story for today, we hear about John's work. (Matthew 3:1-12; Mark 1:1-8; Luke 3:1-18; John 1:19-28)

John lived a simple life in the desert. His clothes were made of camel's hair and he wore a leather belt around his waist. For food, he ate locusts and wild honey. People from all around came to hear John and be baptized by him in the waters of the River Jordan.

"Turn away from sin," he told those who gathered to listen. "The Kingdom of God is soon to come."

Some people thought that John was really the Messiah, the holy one God had promised to send. But John told them that he was the one the prophet Isaiah had spoken about, the one who would prepare the way for the Messiah. John said, "He who is coming after me is much greater than I. I am not even worthy to untie the straps of his sandals."

SHARE

John the Baptist made it clear that people must reform their lives in order to be saved. They must —as it has become popular to say—"be born again." Such an experience is rather like driving into the setting sun and suddenly making a U-turn. The light that had blinded and confused now illuminates and shows the way; we see clearly again. Lent is a time to review our life direction, individually and as a family. As a family, when have we hardened our hearts toward a person, group, or class of people? How can we reform? As individuals, when have we been blinded by the demands of work, self-concern, chemical dependency? How can we reform during this season of Lent?

FOLLOW UP

Hug one another, honestly admitting your sorrow for any hurts and asking for forgiveness.

Seek forgiveness and reconciliation through your church.

Make a personal commitment to change one thing about your life that you know is damaging your relationship with God.

Describe, in pictures or words, how you like people to act at home. Display the pictures and written descriptions where they will be seen by the whole family.

CREATE IN ME A CLEAN HEART, O GOD; AND RENEW
A RIGHT SPIRIT WITHIN ME. (Psalm 51:10, KJV)

Lord, help us to know ourselves:
what we are and what we can become.
Enable us to see what is good within us
and to be thankful for our strengths.
But let us also see the flaws
which keep us from being all that we might be.
Help us look inward with honesty
and be willing to change
whatever is in need of changing.
We ask this in Jesus' name. Amen.

JOHN BAPTIZES JESUS

Jesus appears to have lived a private life as a carpenter in Nazareth. When he was about 30 years old, he began his public ministry. One of the things he did to prepare himself was to be baptized. In our story for today, we hear about Jesus' baptism. (Matthew 3:13-17; Mark 1:9-11; Luke 3:21-22)

Jesus came from Galilee to the River Jordan and asked John to baptize him.

John was surprised by this request. "I should not be baptizing you," he said. "It is you who should be baptizing me."

Still, Jesus insisted. So John did as he was asked and baptized Jesus in the waters of the River Jordan.

When Jesus came up from the water, the heavens opened and the Spirit of God descended on him. Then a voice from heaven said, "This is my beloved Son, with whom I am well pleased."

SHARE

Baptism is an especially important event in family life. Most of us are baptized as infants, so it's up to parents to make all the arrangements—to decide when and where the baptism will take place and to select sponsors. Then we are received into a community of believers. What events surrounded each of our baptisms? (Name dates, places, sponsors, others in attendance, clothing, gifts.) How do the names our parents give us reflect parental love? What do our nicknames say about us?

FOLLOW UP

Attend a baptismal ceremony at your church. Sit up close so children can see clearly what is happening.

Look up the meanings of the names of all your family members.

Draw a large tree on a piece of wrapping paper or sheet of tagboard. Draw pictures of everyone in the family and place the pictures on the tree.

A NEW HEART I WILL GIVE YOU, AND A NEW SPIRIT I WILL PUT WITHIN YOU. (Ezekiel 36:26, RSV)

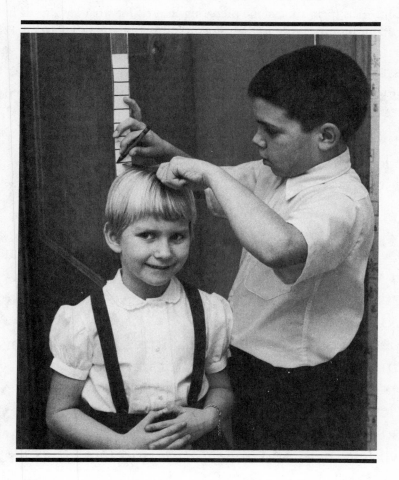

Lord, at baptism we were welcomed
into our church community.
As infants, we were too young to speak for ourselves,
so our parents spoke for us.
As we grow older, it is up to us
not only to speak for ourselves
but to become responsible people as well.
Help us say no to evil, Lord,
and to live in such a way
that we reveal your love through our words
and through our actions. Amen.

JESUS IS TEMPTED

After his baptism, Jesus spent time alone preparing himself for what lay ahead. In our story for today, we hear about his experience in the wilderness. (Matthew 4:1-11; Mark 1:12-13; Luke 4:1-13)

After Jesus was baptized, the Holy Spirit led him into the wilderness. There Jesus stayed for forty days and forty nights. All during that time he fasted. At the end of the forty days, when he was very hungry, the devil said to him, "If you are the Son of God, command these stones to become loaves of bread."

Jesus answered, "It is written that people do not live by bread alone but by every word that comes from the mouth of God."

Then the devil took Jesus up to a high place and said, "If you are the Son of God, throw yourself down, for it is written that angels have charge over you and will not let you be harmed."

Jesus answered, "Again it is written that you shall not tempt the Lord your God."

Once more the devil took Jesus up to a high place. This time he showed him all the power and riches of the world. "I will give you all these things if you will fall down and worship me," the devil said.

To this Jesus replied, "Begone, Satan! For it is written, you shall worship and serve only the Lord your God."

The devil left then, and angels came and tended to Jesus.

SHARE

When we think of temptation, we tend to think of some wrong we've been faced with. Of course we're tempted to do those things that will be hurtful to us and to our neighbors. But aren't we also tempted to do good things? Let's think about times when we considered doing some kindness and then didn't follow through, like calling an old friend with an invitation to lunch or doing a favor for a parent or grandparent, or complimenting someone. Why didn't we do these things when we thought about them? How can we become better at following through when we're tempted to do good?

FOLLOW UP

Follow through on the good actions you've considered doing. Take some family pictures, teach another family member a new skill, redecorate a room, plan a surprise party, join a prayer group, quit smoking, exercise, diet, clean your room.

Spend time alone today, reflecting on your need to say no to evil.

DIRECT MY STEPS AS YOU HAVE PROMISED, LET EVIL WIN NO POWER OVER ME. (Psalm 119:133, JB)

Be our refuge and our strength, Lord.
Help us use our time well
and make choices that are pleasing to you.
Give us the courage to stand up for our convictions,
the strength to do what is right,
and the will to reject what is wrong.
We ask this in Jesus' name. Amen.

A PLEASANT VOICE MULTIPLIES FRIENDS, AND A GRACIOUS TONGUE MULTIPLIES COURTESIES.
(Sirach 6:5, RSV)

PRAY

Leader: Let's join hands and be quiet for a moment before we begin our prayer. If we have worries, let's put them aside and prepare ourselves to be happy together. (Pause for a moment.)

Dear Lord, we gather in your name on this second Sunday in Lent. We know that you hear all prayers. Today we are going to speak to you in our own words.

Would anyone like to ask God for his help this week? (Wait for a response.)

Would anyone like to thank God for anything? (Wait for a response.)

Would anybody like to pray for another person? (Wait for a response.)

Thank you, Lord, for listening to our prayers. Amen.

READ SCRIPTURE

First Reader: Some people brought a woman to Jesus. They told Jesus that the woman had done bad things and deserved to die. Their plan was to stone her to death. The people asked Jesus what he thought about this. They really hoped that his answer would be something they could use against him. Here is the story as John tells it in his Gospel:

> Jesus bent down and started writing on the ground with his finger. As [the people] persisted with their question, he looked

up and said, "If there is one of you who has not sinned, let him be the first to throw a stone at her." Then he bent down and wrote on the ground again. When [the people] heard this they went away one by one. . . until Jesus was left alone with the woman, who remained standing there. He looked up and said, "Woman, where are they? Has no one condemned you?" "No one, sir," she replied. "Neither do I condemn you," said Jesus, "go away and don't sin any more."

John 8: 2-11, JB

SHARE AND REFLECT

Second Reader: In this story we see some of the qualities that made Jesus such a special person. Although the people tried to trick him, Jesus didn't get into an argument or raise his voice. He thought for a moment and then said something that made the people look not at the woman's sins but at their own lives and the wrongs they themselves had committed. One by one, they drifted away until only Jesus and the woman remained. What did Jesus do then? He didn't scold; he didn't accuse. Instead he said, "Neither do I condemn you. Go away, and don't sin any more."

Today we're going to talk about the "Voice of Love" and the many ways we use our voices.

When do we fail to use the voice of love? Do we argue angrily? Gossip? Speak sarcastically?

How do we feel about ourselves after we fail to use the voice of love?

How can we use our voices to restore peace?

Let's look back and think of one person who has been a voice of love in our lives. What was special about that person? Are we passing on to others what that person passed on to us? If not, why not?

CLOSE WITH A PRAYER

Leader: For our closing prayer today, let's all speak with one voice as we say the Lord's Prayer together.

FOLLOW UP

Extend your family time together by doing one or more of the following activities.

Voice your love for one another. Often in family life we neglect to express what we like about our son, daughter, spouse, mother, father, sister, brother. Sit in a circle. The leader turns to the person to the right and says aloud one nice thing about that person. The one who receives the compliment then turns to the right and says one nice thing about that person. Continue until all have had a turn; then reverse and go to the left. Doesn't it feel good to hear the voice of love?

Begin a cassette-tape library. Interview the oldest member of the family and record his or her thoughts. Parents, make tapes for your children, telling the story of their early years: what they were like, humorous incidents, how much they were enjoyed.

Read for the blind. Many blind students need their texts recorded. For information, check with a local or state organization for the blind.

Work on saying "I love you" to the various members of your family. If you find this difficult, John Powell offers much to help you in the paperback entitled *Why Am I Afraid to Love?* (Argus Communications).

TREATS

Serve lemonade or tea with honey—treats for the throat and voice.

JESUS IS REJECTED IN NAZARETH

After spending forty days in the wilderness, Jesus returned to Galilee. Word about him spread throughout the region, and he was invited to teach in the synagogues. In our story for today, we hear what happened when he visited his home town. (Luke 4:16-30; Matthew 13:53-58; Mark 6:1-5)

Jesus came to Nazareth where he had grown up. As was his custom, he went to the synagogue on the Sabbath. There he was handed the book of the prophet Isaiah. He read this passage:

"The Spirit of the Lord is upon me, because he has anointed me to preach good news to the poor. He has sent me to proclaim release to the captives, to give sight to the blind, to free those who are oppressed, and to proclaim the year of the Lord's favor."

When Jesus had finished the reading, there were some people who doubted that he could be the holy one sent by God.

Jesus said to them, "I say to you, a prophet is not accepted in his own country."

When Jesus went on to explain more about the Scriptures, the people did not want to listen. They became angry and forced him out of the city. Some people even wanted to throw him off a high hill, but Jesus walked through the crowd and went away safely.

SHARE

Many people who saw and heard Jesus in person rejected his message. Other well-known people have also experienced rejection. Eleanor Roosevelt did because of her appearance. Margaret Mitchell's book *Gone with the Wind* was rejected by many publishers. Martin Luther King, Jr., felt the sting of rejection because of the color of his skin. Yet in spite of rejection, each succeeded. We can, too. Although we may not become world renowned, we can become better people. After experiencing rejection, we might well become more understanding, loving, compassionate. How does it feel to be a klutz at some game or sport? To be turned down for a badly-wanted job? To fall short of a goal? How can rejection make us stronger?

FOLLOW UP

Take a family trip to the library. Look especially for biographies of those who have overcome rejection and other obstacles. Find books suitable for all ages.

Seek a support group for any family member needing one.

Set aside family time to do things at which all can succeed: walking, working jigsaw puzzles, gardening, making pizza, singing.

*COME TO ME, ALL YOU WHO ARE WEARY AND FIND
LIFE BURDENSOME, AND I WILL REFRESH YOU.
(Matthew 11:28, NAB)*

Lord, being rejected hurts.
No matter how hard others try to comfort us,
we feel empty and alone.
Life loses its zest; food loses its taste.
And it seems as if the sun will never brighten our days again.
Lord, let those of us who have survived the pain of rejection
understand the pain of others.
Show us how to be compassionate;
help us care for those who are hurting and alone. Amen.

THE CALLING OF SIMON, JAMES, AND JOHN

Jesus knew he would need help in spreading the good news of God's love. In our story for today, he invites three fishermen to help him in his work. (Luke 5:1-11; Matthew 4:18-22; Mark 1:16-20)

Jesus was at the Sea of Galilee where a crowd pressed so close to him that he was backed to the water's edge. He stepped into a boat owned by a fisherman named Simon. Sitting down in the boat, Jesus talked to the people on shore. When he had finished, he said to Simon, "Put out into the deep water and let down your nets for a catch."

"Master," Simon protested, "we fished all night and got nothing!" But then he said, "At your word I will let down the nets."

When Simon did as Jesus said, he caught so many fish that the nets were ripping. His partners had to come to help him, and they filled both boats with fish. When Simon saw the size of the catch, he was amazed. Dropping to his knees, he said, "Depart from me, O Lord, for I am a sinful man."

"Do not be afraid," Jesus said. "From now on you will be catching people."

When the fishermen brought their boats to land, they left everything they had and followed Jesus.

SHARE

Although the disciples gave up the work they had been doing and followed Jesus, they were not free of worry, nor did they suddenly change into saintly people. At times they grumbled, had doubts, worried about meals, argued with one another. They responded much as we do when we're invited to do work we're not sure we want to be involved in or can handle. Let's talk about work that might be waiting for us to do. In our church, who will lead the choir? Teach? Usher? Operate a nursery? Serve as future pastors? What can we do? In government, who will lobby for the poor? Stand up for victims of crime? Fight for human rights? What can we do? In our neighborhood, who will provide quality day care? Counsel teens? Bolster families? Beautify the environment? What can we do?

FOLLOW UP

Encourage open discussion of aspirations. (Remember that girls deserve the same opportunities as boys.)

Invite your pastor to dinner and discuss the many ways people may hear and respond to the Lord's call.

Find jobs young children can do at home. Praise them for their work.

CHOOSE THIS DAY WHOM YOU WILL SERVE...AS FOR ME AND MY HOUSE, WE WILL SERVE THE LORD.
(Joshua 24:15, RSV)

Lord, open my eyes so that I may see
whatever you have in mind for me.
Am I to give others a gentle touch?
Spend time with those I love so much?
Explore the wonders of your creation?
Run for office to serve the nation?
Will I harvest the seeds others have sown?
Will I be famous, or mostly unknown?
Lord, open my eyes that I may see
whatever you have in mind for me. Amen.

JESUS CURES THE PARALYTIC

Jesus healed people's bodies. He also healed their spirits by forgiving them their sins. In our story for today, we hear about a man who was healed in both body and spirit. (Luke 6:17-26; Mark 2:1-12; Matthew 9:1-8)

When Jesus was in the town of Capernaum, so many of his followers surrounded the house he was staying in that no one could even get to the door. Some men arrived carrying a paralyzed man on his bed. They wanted to bring the paralytic to Jesus, but they could not move through the crowd. Undaunted, they went up on the roof and found a way to lower the man and his bed into the middle of the room.

When Jesus saw the faith of these men, he looked at the paralytic and said, "Your sins are forgiven."

This upset some of the people. "Who but God can forgive sins?" they wondered.

"Why do you question?" Jesus said to them. "Which is easier to say, 'Your sins are forgiven,' or 'Rise and walk'?"

So that the people would know he really had authority to forgive sins, Jesus said to the paralytic, "Rise, take up your bed and go home."

Immediately the man rose and picked up his bed. On his way home, he gave thanks to God. All who saw what happened were impressed and praised God, saying, "We have seen strange things today."

SHARE

The story about Jesus' cure of the paralytic reminds us of the importance of healing. Lent is a time to examine our physical, mental, and spiritual selves, a time to get well. We don't have to be doctors to recognize the need for healing. Loneliness, greed, stress, anger, a refusal to take time for others—all are symptoms of an ailing way of life. Only if we recognize and admit our need, can we be healed. What does our family do to maintain physical health? Mental health? Spiritual health?

FOLLOW UP

Families, as well as couples, need both time together and time apart. As a family plan your next vacation. As parents consider weekends away, sometimes together, sometimes separately.

Exercise more: walk, bowl, jog, swim, golf, lift weights.

Read a book by an inspirational author such as Thomas Merton or Catherine Marshall.

Give special attention to one another on a one-to-one basis.

I AM FEARFULLY AND WONDERFULLY MADE.
(Psalm 139:14, KJV)

Lord, we are indeed wonderfully made.
When we're enjoying good health,
we give little thought to illness.
But when we're sick,
all we can think about is getting well again.
We pray especially for those people
whose illness and pain never leave.
Give them the strength to meet each new day
with renewed courage.
And when they become irritable or depressed,
help us meet their needs with kindness and patience.
We ask this in Jesus' name. Amen.

JESUS AND THE TAX COLLECTORS

The men who collected taxes for Rome were despised members of the communities in which they lived. In our story for today, we see that Jesus' love extended even to these people. (Mark 2:14-17; Matthew 9:9-13; Luke 5:27-32)

A man by the name of Levi became one of Jesus' followers. Levi was a tax collector, and so were many of his friends.

One day Levi had a special meal at his house. He invited his tax-collecting friends and others considered to be sinners. He also invited Jesus and his disciples.

Some of the people who saw Jesus eating with Levi and his friends complained to the disciples. "Why does he eat with these bad people?" they asked one another.

Jesus overheard the comments. "People who are healthy do not need a doctor," he said, "but sick people do. I have come to call sinners, not the self-righteous."

SHARE

Many of us find it easiest to stay close to those most like ourselves. The young prefer the young. The rich associate with the rich, athletes with athletes. Although it may be comfortable being with our peers, it limits us and keeps us from seeing others as distinct individuals who—once we get to know their feelings and ideas, hopes and dreams—are not so different after all. Jesus challenges us to see a broader world, to reach out and be concerned about the poor, the old, the truly needy. Let's consider our family's attitudes. Do we have a superior attitude at school, in church or on the job? Do we look down on certain groups or types of people? What would Jesus have to say about our attitudes? What can we do to change these attitudes?

FOLLOW UP

Consider "adopting" a grandparent in the nearest nursing home. Really get to know this person through regular visits. If possible, have your adopted grandparent come to your home for an occasional meal. Perhaps include him or her in holiday celebrations.

Open your home to a foreign exchange student.

Go through your closets and give away clothes that are still in good condition but that you could do without.

OPEN WIDE YOUR HAND TO YOUR BROTHER, TO
THE NEEDY AND TO THE POOR, IN THE LAND.
(Deuteronomy 15:11, RSV)

Lord, we know that we are called to reach out
to our sisters and brothers.
We want to be compassionate people,
but it's so easy to find excuses,
to turn away from those in need.
Help us hear the silent pleas of friends
who are hurting emotionally.
Show us a way to serve those
who feel that life is hopeless
and that they are forgotten.
We ask this in Jesus' name. Amen.

LOVE YOUR ENEMIES

In our story for today, Jesus asks us to love even those people who appear not to deserve it. (Luke 6:27-35; Matthew 5:43-48)

"Love your enemies and do good to those who hate you," Jesus told the people. "Bless those who curse you and pray for those who do you harm. If someone strikes you on one cheek, offer the other. If anyone takes away your coat, give your shirt as well. Give to all who beg from you, and when you lend, do not expect to be repaid. Treat others the way you would have them treat you."

Jesus went on to explain what he meant. "If you love those who love you, what credit is that to you?" he asked. "Even sinners love those who love them. And if you do good to those who do good to you, what credit is that to you? Even sinners do that. And if you lend to those from whom you expect to receive, what credit is that to you? Even sinners do as much. Love your enemies and do good. When you lend, expect nothing in return and your reward will be great. You will be children of God."

SHARE

We live in a violent world. It has always been so. People fought one another during the time that Jesus walked the earth; and today—some 2000 years after his message of love—there appears to be a rising tide of hatred and violence. Every newspaper has story after story about violent acts. Attacks are made on popes and presidents, on the old and the young, on the rich and the poor. What events can turn people into enemies? Has our family made any enemies? What steps can we take to mend these relationships?

FOLLOW UP

Talk freely about school, work, and play experiences that involve strife. Help one another find ways to resolve problems with people who bully or threaten.

Pray regularly for those who suffer at the hands of their enemies.

Express your attitude toward violence on TV by writing letters to the networks that carry the violent shows or the companies which sponsor them.

ABOVE ALL HOLD UNFAILING YOUR LOVE FOR ONE ANOTHER. (1 Peter 4:8, RSV)

Lord, help us see our enemies
as people who hurt within themselves,
whose anger is real,
and who need love just as much as we do.
Give us the strength to pray for our enemies
not just once, but again and again.
Grant us the grace to forgive and forget.
We ask this in Jesus' name. Amen.

YOUR REWARD WILL BE GREAT

In our story for today, Jesus tells us how we should respond to the faults of others. (Luke 6:36-38; Matthew 7:1-5)

"Be merciful as your heavenly Father is merciful," Jesus said.

"Do not judge and you will not be judged.

"Do not condemn and you will not be condemned.

"Pardon and you will be pardoned.

"Give and it will be given you.

"For whatever you give will be given back to you many times over."

SHARE

Some of the things we do thoughtlessly are both unfair and unchristian. Judging others is but one example. Most of us have plenty of experience at it. We make snap judgments about everything from the way people look to the clothes they wear, from the cars they drive to the neighborhoods in which they live. Lent is a good time to reflect on such habits and to try to change them. Let's discuss some of the ways we've judged others recently. How have we judged a schoolmate? Neighbor? Co-worker? Politician? Pastor? Why did we think it necessary to judge someone else? When and how did we learn to judge by "first impressions"? How do snap judgments hurt the people we judge? How do they hurt us? How can we keep from making snap judgments?

FOLLOW UP

Give each person an old magazine. Tear out all the ads that include people. Spread out the pictures and study them carefully. Discuss what each ad "says" about people and how your family is influenced by the ad's message.

Draw a flower with many petals on a sheet of construction paper. On each petal, print a word that describes inner qualities we admire in others but may not immediately see. Display the work in the kitchen.

Pray for forgiveness for past judgments of others.

LET US NO MORE PASS JUDGMENT ON ONE ANOTHER. *(Romans 14:13, RSV)*

Inspire us, Lord, to look beyond first impressions.
Help us realize
that a child may be so love-filled
we are shamed by comparison;
that a short person may stand tall
in all the ways that really matter;
that the man with the faltering walk
may be stubbornly fighting a disabling disease;
that the woman in the outdated clothes
may be working for less than the minimum wage.
Lord, help us to see with our hearts
instead of judging with our eyes. Amen.

LET US NOT GROW WEARY IN WELL-DOING, FOR IN DUE SEASON WE SHALL REAP, IF WE DO NOT LOSE HEART. (Galatians 6:9, RSV)

GATHER

Gather the family around a table or wherever you can all be comfortable and have eye contact with one another. Be close enough so that you can easily join hands while praying. Establish a relaxed and informal atmosphere. Choose a leader and two readers.

LIGHT A CANDLE

Light a candle as a sign to everyone that the time you spend together has special significance—you are placing yourselves in the presence of the Lord.

SING

Sing "This Little Light of Mine" on page 11 or another song of your choice that is appropriate for Lent.

PRAY

Leader: Let's join hands as we turn to God in prayer.

Lord, as we gather on this third Sunday in Lent, we thank you for all the good things in our lives. You have blessed us in many ways. As we continue on our lenten journey of love, we ask that you help us share our blessings with others. Let our friendly actions and kind deeds speak of our love for you and for one another. Amen.

READ SCRIPTURE

First Reader: Jesus lived a life of love. He reached out to people, touching them, listening to them, and caring about their problems. Jesus' first miracle appears to have been an act of love for his mother and for a bride and groom celebrating their marriage. In the words of John we read:

> There was a wedding at Cana in Galilee. The mother of Jesus was there, and his disciples had also been invited. When they ran out of wine, . . . the mother of Jesus said to him, "They have no wine." Jesus said, "Woman, why turn to me? My hour has not come yet." His mother said to the servants, "Do whatever he tells you." There were six stone water jars standing there . . . : each could hold twenty or thirty gallons. Jesus said to the servants, "Fill the jars with water," and they filled them to the brim. "Draw some out now," he told them "and take it to the steward." They did this; the steward tasted the water, and it had turned to wine.

> *John 2:1-9, JB*

SHARE AND REFLECT

Second Reader: By turning the water into wine, Jesus kept the bride and groom from being embarrassed. In Scripture we find that Jesus does not just talk about love. He teaches it by his example. A Christian minister named Kagawa followed Jesus' example of love. He spent much of his life working for the needy in his native Japan. But he must have felt there was still more he could do when he wrote: I read once / in a book / that a man / called Christ / went about / doing good. / It distresses me / that I am / so easily satisfied / with just / going about.

Today we are going to talk about the "Deed of Love" and ways we might go about "doing good" instead of just "going about."

Is a deed of love something that takes time and a lot of effort? Could a deed of love be something as simple as an encouraging word or a friendly smile?

Mother Teresa of Calcutta says that if we Christians did one loving deed every day, we could transform the world. What do you think of this idea?

CLOSE WITH A PRAYER

Leader: Dear Lord, it's easier to talk about love than to act it out in daily life. We ask that you show us ways to put our words into action. Help us live as Jesus did by practicing what we preach; help us mark this week's lenten journey with deeds of love. Amen.

FOLLOW UP

Extend your family time together by doing one or more of the following activities.

Write the name of each family member on a slip of paper. Draw names. Sometime during the week, do a deed of love for the person whose name you drew.

Does someone in the family do all, or most of the household chores? If so, work out a plan to share such tasks as shopping, cooking, cleaning.

Most of us know someone who is old, alone, lonely. With your family, think of such a person and decide on something you could do. Pay a visit? Take a plant? Bring some baked goods? Invite him or her to your home for a meal?

Babysit free of charge for someone who does not get out often.

TREATS

Serve a dessert that is a family favorite. Plan ahead and select one that requires effort to prepare and in effect says, "I love you and I'm glad to be able to do something special for you."

A BLIND MAN

Jesus' reputation spread. Everywhere he went, people crowded around. Some wanted only to hear his words; others wanted his healing touch. In our story for today, we hear about a man who asked Jesus to give him his sight. (Luke 18:35-43; Matthew 20:29-34; Mark 10:46-52)

A blind beggar sat beside the road that led to the city of Jericho. When he heard a crowd approaching, he asked what was happening.

"It's Jesus," someone told him. "Jesus of Nazareth is coming this way."

Upon hearing this, the blind man cried out, "Jesus, Jesus, have mercy on me!"

Those who stood near the blind beggar tried to quiet him, but he only cried louder. "Jesus! Jesus, have mercy on me!"

Jesus stopped and asked that the man be brought to him. Then he said, "What do you want?"

"Lord," the blind man pleaded, "let me have my sight."

Jesus said to him, "Receive your sight. Your faith has made you well."

At that moment, the blind man was able to see. His eyes were opened, and he followed Jesus, giving thanks to God.

SHARE

After Jesus restored his sight, the blind man saw everything in a new way. We might say that he had renewed vision as well as being able to see in the more usual way. Anyone who has been temporarily sightless understands this. When use of the eyes is restored, we appreciate color and detail, but we also have vision. We think anew and have greater appreciation of life's possibilities. When do we become blind to the needs of our family or to the good things our life together brings? When this happens, what must we do to see anew all the possibilities of our family life?

FOLLOW UP

With permission, blindfold someone and lead that person around the house for two or three minutes. Then remove the blindfold and discuss the experiences of "being blind" and having sight restored.

Read a book about the life of Helen Keller.

Take care of any eye problems so that everyone in the family may see as clearly as possible.

*THE THINGS WHICH ARE SEEN ARE TEMPORAL; BUT
THE THINGS WHICH ARE NOT SEEN ARE ETERNAL.
(2 Corinthians 4:18, KJV)*

There are times, Lord, when we have sight,
but no vision.
We see the tasks that demand to be done,
but not the goal.
We are overwhelmed; something is wrong.
At first we may not realize it,
but there are signs that we don't see life
the way you intend us to.
We overeat, overdrink, overyell.
Lord, grant us the wisdom to unclutter our lives
so that we have a clearer vision
of the way you want us to live. Amen.

THE PARABLE OF THE SOWER

Jesus often told stories called "parables" to help people understand the truths he was teaching. In our story for today, we hear one of his parables about seeds. (Luke 8:4-15; Matthew 13:1-9; Mark 4:1-9)

"A sower went out to sow his seed," Jesus said. "Some of the seeds fell along the path and birds came and ate them. Some fell on rocky ground and could not grow. Some dropped among thorns that choked out the plants. Others fell on good soil. They grew and produced plentiful crops."

Jesus looked around at the people and said, "Those who have ears to hear, let them hear."

The story puzzled the disciples and they asked Jesus to explain it. He went on to say, "The seed is like the word of God. Some people hear, but do not believe. For others, the word is like the seeds that fall on rocky ground. They believe for awhile, but the word does not take root. For still others, God's word is choked out by the cares and pleasures of life. But there are those for whom the word is like the seeds sown in good soil. They hear it and grow in goodness and love."

SHARE

The parable that Jesus told is easily understood by anyone who has ever tried to grow plants from seeds. The seeds must be tended; they need water, sunlight, fertilizer, space in which to grow. Those of us who attend church regularly and read Scripture have God's word planted in us many times in a single year. What is the result? Are we allowing the word to grow within us? Do we refuse to let some ideas take root? Which ideas have taken hold in our family? (Consider how you love, serve, forgive, listen, share.)

FOLLOW UP

Provide each family member with a suitable Bible.

Make a special effort to practice the Golden Rule for one full week without mentioning it to anyone.

Plant and tend some seeds.

LISTEN TO MY VOICE; THEN I WILL BE YOUR GOD AND YOU SHALL BE MY PEOPLE. (Jeremiah 7:23, NAB)

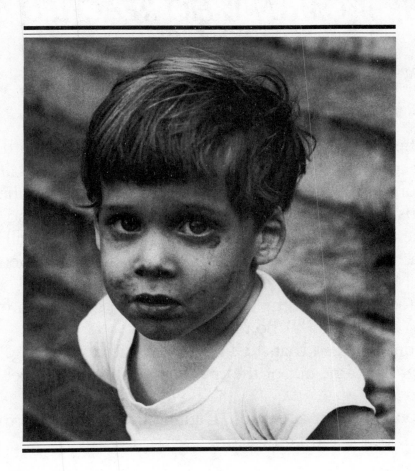

Lord, we want very much to be your people.
Please forgive us when we are careless
in our relationship with you—
when we hear your word,
but do not listen as carefully as we could;
when we hear your word,
but do not act on it as completely as we should;
when we hear your word,
but neglect to serve others and do good.
Lord, we want very much to be your people.
We ask that you forgive us when we fail to act on your word
and that you strengthen us to try over and over again. Amen.

THE WOMAN WHO REACHED OUT TO JESUS

Jesus reached out to suffering people, and they also reached out to him. In our story for today, we hear about the healing of a woman who had great faith. (Mark 5:25-34; Matthew 9:18-26; Luke 8:40-56)

Among the people who followed Jesus was a woman who had been sick for years. Even though she had gone to many doctors and spent all her money, she didn't get any better. The woman had heard stories about Jesus and how he healed people. Coming up behind him in the crowd, she thought, "If only I can touch his garment, I will be made well." Reaching out, she touched the hem of his cloak. Even before she pulled back her hand, she knew she had been healed.

Jesus, too, knew that the power to heal had gone forth from him. He turned and asked, "Who touched me?"

The woman feared that she had done something wrong. Trembling, she came out of the crowd and fell at Jesus' feet. "I did," she admitted.

Jesus looked at her and said, "Daughter, your faith has made you well. Go in peace and be healed."

SHARE

People who put their faith in gold believe that they will become richer than they are today. It is somewhat the same for those who put their faith in God. They, too, believe they will become richer. There is one big difference, however. The value of gold is uncertain, while faith in God leads to eternal life. Let's talk about having faith. How does it feel to have faith? Have any experiences tested our faith? If so, how did we respond? In what ways does faith change as we grow older?

FOLLOW UP

Pray especially that those who have abandoned their faith will experience a renewal of belief.

Discuss how people learn to love and trust. (Consider infancy through the teen years.)

Draw pictures or write descriptions of people you trust. Send a note of encouragement to your pastor.

FAITH IS THE SUBSTANCE OF THINGS HOPED FOR,
THE EVIDENCE OF THINGS NOT SEEN.
(Hebrews 11:1, KJV)

Lord, whenever we feel discouraged
and faith falters,
help us turn to you.
You are our source of hope.
Renew our faith so that we might pass
through the dark moments of life
knowing that you are with us always. Amen.

JESUS SENDS FORTH THE DISCIPLES

Jesus prepared the disciples to help him with his work. In our story for today, we hear about their mission. (Matthew 10:5-15; Luke 9:1-6; Mark 6:7-13)

"Take no money with you when you go," Jesus told the disciples. "Take no extra sandals or clothing."

The disciples surely understood that they were to teach people about God's love and to care for those who were sick or troubled. But how were they to get along without money? Where would they stay? What would they eat?

Jesus went on to say, "When you enter a new town, search out people you can trust and stay with them. Give a special blessing of peace to the homes of kind and honest people."

Jesus knew there would be towns where the disciples would not be welcome. He said, "If you come to such a place, leave and go somewhere else. But do not stop spreading the good news about God's love."

After Jesus had told them what they were to do, the disciples left and went through the villages, preaching and healing everywhere.

SHARE

Some Christian denominations are more commited to a personal witnessing ministry than others. They use TV, printed materials and door-to-door witnessing as part of their outreach. What about our church? How active are we in spreading God's word? Seeking new members? Sponsoring missionaries? Let's discuss our attitudes. What do we think about the work of missionaries? What financial support do we give them? What other kinds of support might we give? Are we ever embarrassed or hesitant to speak out for the Lord? If so, why?

FOLLOW UP

Become more active in some form of missionary work.

Become involved in a social-action program sponsored by your church. If there is no such program, take an active part in getting one started.

Take a class or join a study group to learn more about your faith so you'll be better prepared to share it.

GO INTO THE WHOLE WORLD AND PROCLAIM THE GOOD NEWS. (Mark 16:15, NAB)

Lord, when it's time to stand up and be witnesses,
we're not always as confident as we'd like to be.
Sometimes we're embarrassed to speak out in your name.
Sometimes we hesitate to act upon our beliefs.
Lord, help us overcome any embarrassment or fear we have.
Inspire us to be less hesitant
to pass along your love to others. Amen.

BIRDS OF THE AIR
AND LILIES OF THE FIELD

God gives us life and asks for our trust. In our story for today, Jesus tells us that if we trust in God, we need not be anxious about the necessities of life. (Matthew 6:26-34; Luke 12:22-31)

"Do not worry about what you will eat or what you will drink," Jesus said. "Look at the birds of the air. They do not sow seeds or harvest crops, yet God feeds them. Are you not of more value than they?"

Then Jesus went on to say, "Why are you worried about clothes? Look at the lilies of the field. They do not work or spin, yet even King Solomon in his royal robes was not dressed as splendidly as they. Does not the God who clothes the lilies of the field care even more about you? So do not be worried about what you will eat or what you will wear. Your heavenly Father knows you need these things. Seek first to live a life pleasing to God and then you will have what you need."

SHARE

We have all met people who feel the world owes them a living. When they don't have all they want, they suggest that God has failed to provide. God doesn't fail. People do. God has provided us with talents and strengths to enable us to meet our needs. How has the Lord provided for us to meet the needs of our family? Each of us has abilities. What are they? How can we develop them more fully?

FOLLOW UP

God created the world, and we are its caretakers. Make a bird feeder by cutting out the sides of a half-gallon milk carton, leaving a tray about one inch deep for birdseed. Use string to hang the bird feeder outdoors.

Provide nesting materials—bits of yarn, cotton balls, straw—where birds can find them.

Develop a specific plan to relieve stress. Read a book about relaxation techniques; exercise; eat properly.

CAN ANY OF YOU LIVE A BIT LONGER BY WORRYING ABOUT IT? *(Matthew 6:27, GN)*

Lord, why do we worry so much?
We worry about health, money, death, taxes;
we worry about the weather and the way we look;
we even worry about worrying!
Could worrying be an excuse
to avoid getting on with life?
Does worrying prevent us from taking the risks
that come with living life to the full?
Help us, Lord, to put more trust in you.
Take away our self-concern
and replace it with concern for others.
Then send us forth in peace to love and to serve. Amen.

THE LOAVES AND THE FISH

Jesus cared for people in many ways. In our story for today, we see him satisfying the hunger of a crowd. (Matthew 14:13-21; Mark 6:30-44; Luke 9:10-17; John 6:1-13)

Jesus and his disciples went off to the countryside to be alone for a time. But when the people heard where he was, they came looking for him. Jesus welcomed them and spoke about the Kingdom of God.

Late in the day, the disciples came to Jesus. "This is a lonely place and it is getting dark," they said. Send the people away so that they can go to the villages for food."

"There is no need for them to go away," Jesus said. "*You* give them something to eat."

"How can we?" asked the disciples. "We have only five loaves and two fish."

"Bring them to me," Jesus told them. When the disciples gave Jesus the five loaves and two fish, he looked up to heaven. Then he blessed and broke the loaves and gave them to his disciples. He also divided the two fish. The disciples then passed out the food, and the people in the crowd ate as much as they wanted. After everyone had eaten, the disciples filled twelve baskets with food that was left.

SHARE

Jesus shared his time, his thoughts, his power. Jesus' sharing of the loaves and fish was a miracle. Many people today are skeptical of miracles, and rightly so. But to disbelieve in all miracles is to cut ourselves off from potentially wonderful experiences. Believe in wonders, but don't plan on them; for it seems to be the nature of miracles to occur when least expected! Let's share family experiences about unexpected blessings. When has something pleasing that was totally unexpected happened to us? How did we respond? Was it luck? A blessing? A miracle? Why might people think that miracles occurred in Jesus' time but not today?

FOLLOW UP

Pray privately for others and keep your prayers confidential.

Bake, break, and share a loaf of bread.

Invite friends to your home for a potluck meal.

Share stories or sing with the younger children in your family to help them realize that sharing doesn't necessarily result in the giver having less.

I AM THE LIVING BREAD WHICH HAS COME DOWN FROM HEAVEN. *(John 6:51, JB)*

Lord, you are the only one who can satisfy our spiritual hunger.
Help us prepare ourselves
to share in Communion with our brothers and sisters.
Lead us to accept the invitation
to come to your table often during the remaining days of Lent.
We ask this in Jesus' name. Amen.

LOVE ONE ANOTHER EARNESTLY FROM THE HEART.
(1 Peter 1:22, GN)

PRAY

Leader: Let's join hands as we turn to God in prayer.

Lord, as we gather on this fourth Sunday in Lent we ask that you continue to guide us on our journey of love. Sometimes we succeed in our efforts to be loving people and sometimes we fail. When we fail, keep us from losing heart. Help us renew our efforts to follow Jesus' command to love one another as we love ourselves. Amen.

READ SCRIPTURE

First Reader: Love is a word that's used in many ways and has different meanings for different people. When we want to get at the true meaning of something, we say we want to get at the heart of it. In one of Paul's letters to the Corinthians, he gets at the heart of love. He writes:

If I speak in the tongues of men and of angels, but have not love, I am a noisy gong or a clanging cymbal. And if I have prophetic powers, and understand all mysteries and all knowledge, and if I have all faith, so as to remove mountains, but have not love, I am nothing. If I give away all I have, . . . but have not love, I gain nothing.

Love is patient and kind; love is not jealous or boastful; it is not arrogant or rude. Love does not insist on its own way; it is not irritable or resentful; it does not rejoice at wrong, but rejoices in the right. Love bears all things, believes all things, hopes all things, endures all things.

1 Corinthians 13:1-7, RSV

SHARE AND REFLECT

Second Reader: The love that Paul speaks about is an ideal. Most of us fall short of this ideal, but we can always keep on trying. Today we're going to talk about the "Heart of Love" and what it means to us and our family.

It has been said that whoever has a heart full of love always has something to give. What does this mean? Who do we know who always has something to give?

Is there anyone we once disliked who is now a friend? What brought about this change of heart?

Families have good days and bad days. What are bad days like? What could we do to turn them around?

CLOSE WITH A PRAYER

Leader: Today we close with the Prayer of St. Francis.

Lord, make me an instrument of your peace.
Where there is hatred, let me sow love;
where there is injury, pardon;
where there is doubt, faith;
where there is despair, hope;
where there is darkness, light;
where there is sadness, joy.
Oh divine master,
grant that I may not so much seek
to be consoled as to console;
to be understood, as to understand;
to be loved, as to love.
For it is in giving that we receive;
it is in pardoning that we are pardoned;
and it is in dying
that we are born to eternal life.

FOLLOW UP

Extend your family time together by doing one or more of the following activities.

Draw or cut out a large paper heart. On it write "Love one another as I have loved you" (John 15:12, RSV). Then have family members write the name or initials of at least three people they are going to pray for during the coming week. Display the heart in a place where it will serve as a daily reminder.

Express your love for one another right now. Give hugs all around.

Music touches the heart in ways that few other things can. If you are a musical family, spend time singing or playing. Or listen to favorite tapes or records.

Read a book that will contribute to your spiritual growth. Consider *Love* by Leo Buscaglia (Fawcett).

This week make a special point of listening to family members. Try to understand the feelings behind their words.

TREATS

If you want to carry out the theme, serve heart-shaped cookies or homemade pretzels (see the recipe on p. 9) made into hearts. Or serve something that's a favorite with the family.

THE GOOD SAMARITAN

In our story for today, Jesus uses a parable to help us understand who our neighbor is. (Luke 10:25-37)

A lawyer asked Jesus what he must do to have eternal life. Jesus told him, "You shall love the Lord your God with all your heart... and your neighbor as yourself."

"And who is my neighbor?" asked the lawyer.

Jesus answered him with this parable: "A man was traveling the lonely road from Jerusalem to Jericho when he was attacked by two robbers. They took all his belongings, beat him until he was half dead and left him beside the road.

"A while later, a priest came down the same road. When he saw the injured man, he crossed to the other side. Later still, a man who served in the Temple came along. He, too, passed by.

"Then a Samaritan came down the road. When he saw the beaten man, he took pity on him. First he cleaned and bandaged his wounds. Then he put him on his own animal and brought him to an inn where he cared for him.

"The next day the Samaritan had to be on his way. Giving the innkeeper some money, he said, 'Take care of this man. Whatever more you spend, I will repay when I come back.' "

When Jesus finished the parable, he turned to the lawyer. "Which of these three do you think proved to be a neighbor?" he asked.

"The one who took pity on the beaten man," replied the lawyer.

Jesus said, "Go and do likewise."

SHARE

Some of the stories Jesus told make us look inward and confront ourselves. The Good Samaritan is such a story. Would we have stopped to help? Not many of us are faced with so dramatic a situation, but we never know when we might have to make a quick, difficult decision about whether to help someone in need. Let's discuss "good Samaritans" in our community. How do neighbors respond to those who are grieving? What local community organizations depend on volunteers? To whose needs do our church groups respond?

FOLLOW UP

Teach a religious education class.

Recycle paper, metal, glass.

Adopt a dog or cat that would otherwise be destroyed.

Pick up litter outside the place where you live.

BE KIND TO ONE ANOTHER....(Ephesians 4:32, RSV)

Lord, anyone who's had car problems
on an expressway or interstate
understands the need for Good Samaritans.
Cars whiz by with drivers looking straight ahead.
We know it's their way of avoiding us
because we've done it countless times ourselves.
Not wanting to get involved is understandable;
it's risky to stop and help a stranger.
So we wait...and wait...and wait.
Until at last someone pulls over and calls, "Need help?"
Lord, in this age of senseless violence
we give special thanks for today's Good Samaritans.
We ask that you bless and keep watch over them. Amen.

MARTHA AND MARY

There are times in our lives when all our attention should be given to the opportunity before us. In our story for today, Jesus reminds a woman what her priorities should be. (Luke 10:38-40)

Jesus entered a village that was the home of two sisters named Martha and Mary. Martha invited Jesus to stop at their house. When Jesus came inside, Martha busied herself serving food. But her sister Mary didn't do anything to help her. Instead, she sat at the feet of Jesus, listening to his teaching.

After a time, Martha got tired of doing all the work and complained to Jesus. "Lord," she said, "do you not care that my sister has left me to serve alone? Tell her to help me."

"Martha, Martha," Jesus answered, "you are anxious and troubled about many things when there is only one thing you need concern yourself with. Mary has chosen the better part, and it shall not be taken from her."

SHARE

Each of us is something like both Martha and Mary. At times, we're concerned about what to eat and when, what our home or workplace looks like, what clothes to wear. At other times, we're concerned about people and anxious to give them our full attention. Let's talk about our family. When are we likely to busy ourselves and neglect the people we love? Are we satisfied with the balance in our lives, or do we need to set some priorities? How would we act if Jesus stopped by?

FOLLOW UP

Make a list of ten goals you share as a family. Star the two or three most important ones. Discuss what you can to do achieve them.

Decide what you could do during the remainder of Lent to better live out your Christian beliefs.

If you're a procrastinator, make a list each day of the three most important things you must do. Then do them *before* getting involved in other activities.

FOR EVERYTHING THERE IS A SEASON, AND A TIME
FOR EVERY MATTER UNDER HEAVEN.
(Ecclesiastes 3:1, RSV)

Lord, we say we want to be in touch with one another,
yet busy ourselves in ways that keep us apart.
We forget that helping a child with homework
may be more important than attending a meeting;
that taking time to listen
may be more important than a neat house;
that visiting a sick friend may be more important
than finishing a project.
Lord, give us the wisdom to recognize
what is most important in our lives
and the strength to seize opportunities
to reach out with love
to those who mean the most to us. Amen.

HOW TO GIVE AND HOW TO PRAY

When we are proud of our actions, it's tempting to let others know about them. In our story for today, Jesus tells us that when it comes to good deeds and prayer, it's enough that God alone knows. (Matthew 6:1-4)

"When you give alms," Jesus said, "do not blow a trumpet so that people will know about it and praise you. Those who do this have already received their reward. When you give alms, do so in secret, not letting your left hand know what your right hand is doing. God who sees in secret will reward you."

Jesus also spoke about how people should pray. He said, "When you pray, do not do it in the synagogues and on the street corners so that others will see you praying. Those who do this have already received their reward. When you pray, go into your room and shut the door. Then do your praying in secret. God who sees in secret will reward you."

SHARE

It's not easy to be charitable anonymously. If we're being honest with ourselves, most of us will admit that we like the praise and pats on the back we get from having our good deeds known. There's nothing wrong with such recognition as long as it doesn't become an end in itself. Lent is a good time to consider whether we act charitably to impress others or to express what we genuinely feel and believe. Let's think about ways our family might give in secret during these remaining days of Lent. Could we give an anonymous cash donation to someone in need? Even a small amount with a note of encouragement might cause the person to smile and go on with new determination. Do we have any possessions that others need badly and that we could do without? Should we share them? How could we do so anonymously?

FOLLOW UP

Set aside five to ten minutes each day to pray in private.

Write family members' names on slips of paper. Draw names and keep the name you draw a secret. Without being asked—or bragging—do something kind for that person every day for a week.

Watch the newspaper for stories about selflessness. Share them with your family.

*LET ANOTHER PRAISE YOU, AND NOT YOUR OWN
MOUTH; A STRANGER, AND NOT YOUR OWN LIPS.*
(Proverbs 27:2, RSV)

How unlike you we are, Lord!
You were born in a lowly manger.
You didn't ask for special treatment.
You turned down the role of king
and chose to serve instead of being served.
Let us learn from your example
and blow our own horn a little more softly.
With your help,
we might even learn to be humble.
We ask this in your name. Amen.

JESUS TEACHES A PRAYER

Jesus often turned to God in prayer. In our story for today, we hear how he taught his disciples the Lord's Prayer. (Luke 11:1-4; Matthew 6:9-13)

The disciples came to Jesus in a certain place where he was praying. When he had finished, they said to him, "Lord, teach us to pray."

Jesus responded, "When you pray, say:
Our Father who art in heaven,
Hallowed be thy name.
Thy kingdom come,
Thy will be done,
On earth as it is in heaven.
Give us this day our daily bread;
And forgive us our trespasses
As we forgive those who trespass against us;
And lead us not into temptation,
But deliver us from evil."

SHARE

Parents are their children's first teachers, and one of the important things they teach is their attitude toward prayer. Let's consider our family's prayer heritage. Parents, what did your parents teach you about prayer? Children, what are your parents teaching you about prayer? Is the same attitude being passed from generation to generation? If not, how is it different? Let's talk about our family's prayer life. Do we pray regularly? If not, let's do so for thirty days. Do we use mainly formal, memorized prayers? Let's try praying more spontaneously, sharing with God what is really in our hearts. Do we try to live our lives in such a way that they become living prayers? Why is Lent a good time to begin?

FOLLOW UP

Make a prayer banner by pasting cutout felt letters on a background of felt or burlap. Use short prayers such as "God bless us" or "God bless our home."

To learn about unceasing prayer, read Ron DelBene's book *The Breath of Life: A Simple Way to Pray* (Winston Press).

Join or form a prayer group.

"ASK AND YOU SHALL RECEIVE; SEEK AND YOU SHALL FIND; KNOCK AND IT SHALL BE OPENED TO YOU." (Luke 11:9, NAB)

I asked God for strength, that I might achieve;
I was made weak, that I might learn humbly to obey.
I asked for health, that I might do greater things;
I was given infirmity that I might do better things.
I asked for riches, that I might be happy;
I was given poverty, that I might be wise.
I asked for power, that I might have the praise of others;
I was given weakness, that I might feel the need of God.
I asked for all things, that I might enjoy life;
I was given life, that I might enjoy all things.
I got nothing that I asked for, but everything I had hoped for.
Almost despite myself, my unspoken prayers were answered.
I am, among all people, most richly blessed.

Prayer of an unknown Confederate soldier

THE LOST SHEEP

God's care is always with us. In our story for today, Jesus uses a parable about a lost sheep to show the extent of God's love and concern. (Luke 15:1-7; Matthew 18:12-14)

"Suppose a shepherd has a hundred sheep and loses one of them," Jesus said. "What does he do? He leaves the ninety-nine in the wilderness and searches until he finds the one that is lost. Upon finding it, he is so happy that he puts it on his shoulders and carries it back home. There he calls his friends and neighbors together and says to them, 'Rejoice with me, for I have found my sheep that was lost.' "

Jesus then went on to explain the parable, saying, "There will be more joy in heaven over one sinner who asks for forgiveness than over ninety-nine people who have no need to be forgiven."

SHARE

A good shepherd is concerned about all the sheep in the flock and will do whatever has to be done to keep them safe. Like the good shepherd, God is concerned about each of us. Even though we may stray, God remains near, always ready to welcome us back. We can see God's loving protection in our own family. Let's consider some of the times when love has made us greatly concerned about someone. Did any of us ever get lost? Has anyone been seriously ill or badly injured? Has one of us stayed out later than expected? If so, what happened? How does it feel to be temporarily separated from our family? From God? What steps can we take to return?

FOLLOW UP

Make it a point this week to spend time alone with someone who is feeling discouraged or rejected.

Draw sheep on construction paper and paste cotton balls on them for texture. Add the words "The Lord Is My Shepherd." Display the work.

Get in touch with someone who has "strayed" from your friendship.

LOOK OUT FOR ONE ANOTHER'S INTERESTS, NOT JUST FOR YOUR OWN. (Philippians 2:4, GN)

Lord, we are a busy family.
Sometimes we are so concerned about ourselves
that we forget to be as interested in one another as we could be.
Help us to slow down a little
and pay attention to each other.
Put words of encouragement in our mouths
so that we praise more quickly than we criticize.
With your loving guidance we can be special people.
We can be good shepherds to one another. Amen.

THE PRODIGAL SON

Of all the stories Jesus told, the parable about a forgiving father is especially well known. In our story for today, we have an indication of how forgiving and loving God is. (Luke 15:11-33)

A young son who wanted to get away from home went to his father and said, "Father, give me my share of the inheritance now instead of later." The father must have had misgivings, but he did as his son asked.

A few days later, the son took all his belongings and traveled to a country far from home. There he wasted his money on wild living. When a terrible famine came upon the land, he was both penniless and friendless, and the only job he could find was tending pigs. He was so hungry he would have eaten the pigs' food, but no one gave him even that.

The son thought a lot about the things he had done wrong and decided to go to his father and apologize. He was still far away when his father saw him coming. Running to his son, he greeted him warmly.

"Father, I have sinned," the son admitted, "and I am no longer worthy to be called your son."

Instead of being angry, the father was filled with joy and forgiveness. He said to his servants, "Bring the best robe and put it on my son. Slip a ring on his finger and shoes on his feet. Then let us celebrate. My son was lost and now he is found."

SHARE

There is no way we can change the past, but we can change our attitudes and begin life anew. Forgiveness frees us to do just that. Such was the experience of the son in today's story. And it can be our experience as well. Let's talk about forgiveness as we know it. In what ways do we seek forgiveness? Do we admit our faults directly? Do we hedge and try to buy forgiveness with gifts or special attention? Do we try to bargain with God? Recall some wrong you did in the past. What feelings did you have? How did you seek forgiveness? How did you feel after being forgiven? Why is forgiveness important in daily family living? Why haven't we really forgiven if we continue to bring the incident up? How can we forgive *and* forget?

FOLLOW UP

Look through magazines and tear out pictures that show people living happily. Make a collage of the pictures and add a title, such as "To Forgive Is to Love."

Sometimes asking for forgiveness is harder than forgiving. Talk about ways to take the first step toward reconciliation. Consider both the person seeking forgiveness and the person who has been wronged.

If you have been holding a grudge against anyone in your family, go to that person in private and seek forgiveness and reconciliation.

FORGIVE, AND YOU SHALL BE FORGIVEN.
(Luke 6:37, RSV)

Lord, as we look back, we remember the people
who cared enough about us to forgive
our foolish behavior and hurtful words.
Parents, teachers, co-workers, students,
brothers and sisters, husband or wife —
these are some of the people with whom
we have had to make peace.
Help us look inward, Lord,
and honestly review our behavior.
If we've held back forgiveness,
guide us to forgive as we have been forgiven.
We ask this in Jesus' name. Amen.

DO NOT BE CONFORMED TO THIS WORLD BUT BE TRANSFORMED BY THE RENEWAL OF YOUR MIND. (Romans 12:2, RSV)

GATHER

Gather the family around a table or wherever you can all be comfortable and have eye contact with one another. Be close enough so that you can easily join hands while praying. Choose a leader and two readers.

LIGHT A CANDLE

Light a candle as a sign to everyone that the time you spend together has special significance — you are placing yourselves in the presence of the Lord.

SING

Sing "This Little Light of Mine" on page 11 or another song of your choice that is appropriate for Lent.

PRAY

Leader: Let's join hands as we turn our hearts and minds to God in prayer.

Lord, as we gather on this fifth Sunday in Lent, we ask that you strengthen our faith. Help us to understand a little better what it means to be one of God's children. As we continue our lenten journey of love, let us feel your presence. Let us know that you are a personal God whose love is always with us. Amen.

READ SCRIPTURE

First Reader: Last Sunday we read part of one of Paul's letters to the Corinthians. In it he wrote about what love should be. The reading for today is from the same letter. Here, Paul writes about changing as we grow.

> When I was a child, I used to talk like a child, and think like a child, and argue like a child, but now I am a man, all childish ways are put behind me.

> *1 Corinthians 13:10-11, JB*

SHARE AND REFLECT

Second Reader: As children grow, they are expected to take on more responsibilities. Some children feel their parents expect too much of them too soon. Others feel they are treated like babies, believing themselves to be more grown-up than anyone realizes.

There are times when it's hard to be a child. There are also times when it's hard to be a parent. But God has given us minds to deal with our problems. This week we are going to talk about the "Mind of Love" and how we can use our minds constructively as we grow and change.

What attitude does our family have toward personal responsibility? Are we expecting too much or too little of one another? (Consider work, home, and school situations.)

Is there some problem—big or small—that we've been unable to resolve because we've refused to talk about it? Could we look at it with the mind of love and find an answer?

What can we do to help family members stretch their minds? Are there courses to be taken, books to be read, talents to be pursued?

Does anyone have a call to use his or her mind to serve God in a religious vocation? If so, how can the family help? Are we all as open as we could be to God's call to serve?

CLOSE WITH A PRAYER

Leader: Dear Lord, help us remember that the mind must be well fed if it is to reach its full potential. Give us the will to choose those movies and books and TV shows which help our minds grow and the strength to avoid those that do not. Guide us in decisions we must make and fill our minds with the spirit of your love. Amen.

FOLLOW UP

Extend your family time together by doing one or more of the following activities.

Hold a brainstorming session to think of as many solutions as you can to any family problem you need to face.

List your favorite TV shows and talk about the content of each. What appeal does the show have? Is it the kind of program you should be watching? (Try to be objective, and allow everyone to voice an opinion.)

Decide on a show that you believe is of high quality. Then write to the TV network on which it appears and thank the people responsible for presenting it.

Make a family trip to the library and check out books on topics you think will be helpful in developing the mind of love.

Take specific steps to calm and/or inspire yourself. Study Christian meditation, go on a retreat, begin an exercise program, join a prayer group.

TREATS

Putting good things into our stomachs as well as our minds does make a difference. Serve fresh fruit as a reminder of this.

THE TALENTS

God gives everyone special gifts and abilities. In our story for today, Jesus tells a parable about making the most of our gifts. (Matthew 25:14-30; Luke 19:11-27)

A man was going on a journey and trusted his servants with his property. Before leaving, he gave his servants sums of money called talents. One received five silver pieces, another two, and a third only one.

The servant who received five silver talents went at once and traded with them and made five more. Likewise, the servant who was given two made two more. But the servant who received one talent buried his money in the ground.

After a long time, the master came back and asked the servants what they had done with the money. The servant who had received five talents came forward with ten. The master said, "Well done! You have been faithful over a little, so I will set you over much."

The servant who had received two talents came forward with four. Again, the master was pleased.

Then the servant who had received one talent came forward. "Master, I was afraid," he said, "and buried my talent in the ground. So all I have is the one you gave me."

The master became angry and told the servant he had not used his talent well. He took it away and gave it to the servant who had turned his five talents into ten.

SHARE

God has gifted all of us with much more than we realize. We have done nothing to deserve or earn what we have been given. But we are responsible for the full development of our gifts. Parents look for signs of the gifts their children may have received. Are they especially good in art? Music? Sports? Math? These are readily understood gifts which we can measure in some way. But there are other gifts that are less easily measured: gifts of faith, love, understanding, compassion. In our troubled world these gifts are desperately in need of development. Let's talk about our family's gifts. How has God gifted each one of us? How do we use our gifts?

FOLLOW UP

Discuss how the world might change if we spent as much time teaching and learning about peace-making as we spend on baseball or other sports.

Pray together for the patience to develop your gifts.

Enroll for instruction in some skill you want to develop.

DO NOT NEGLECT THE GIFT YOU HAVE.
(1 Timothy 4:14, RSV)

Lord, we admire the accomplishments of others,
but we often forget that even an Olympic champion
was once a beginner.
It's not always easy to try new things.
Instead of thinking how good we might become,
we focus on how we might fail.
Help us develop our talents
and enjoy accomplishments when we succeed.
When we fail, give us the humor to laugh at our mistakes
and the will to try again.
We ask this in Jesus' name. Amen.

JESUS AND THE CHILDREN

In our story today, we learn that to belong to the Kingdom of God, we must have child-like qualities—we must be open, teachable, trusting. (Mark 10:13-16; Matthew 19:13-15; Luke 18:15-17)

When Jesus passed through the villages, people left what they were doing to see him in person. Some came because they were interested in what he had to say. Others came hoping to be cured of illnesses. Parents often brought their children so that Jesus might touch them. On one occasion, the disciples tried to keep the children back because they thought the children might bother Jesus.

Jesus saw what was happening and became annoyed. "Do not stop the children," he said. "Let them come to me, for the kingdom of God belongs to such as these. I say to you, if you do not receive the kingdom of God like a child, you will not enter it."

Calling the children to him, Jesus took them in his arms. Then he laid his hands on their heads and blessed them.

SHARE

One of the things we've come to understand about Jesus is that he saw the good, or potential for good, within all people. He looked at ordinary fishermen and recognized their potential as leaders. He spoke with sinners and understood that they might change their ways of living. Jesus recognized the innate goodness in children and did not allow his disciples to separate him from them. Yes, Jesus sees the good in all of us. And he asks that we, in turn, look for that potential in others. Let's talk about our own experiences. How do we go about recognizing the worth of others and encouraging them at home? In school? On the job?

FOLLOW UP

Surprise someone by making an "Award Certificate" that recognizes the good in that person. Consider an award for a babysitter, your mail carrier, your pastor, a grandparent. Depending on the person awarded, you might include a small gift, a tip, a gift certificate, a flower, a picture you drew especially for that person.

Call an old friend you haven't been in touch with lately.

Hold an open house to show appreciation for your good neighbors.

DO NOT WITHHOLD GOOD FROM THOSE TO WHOM IT IS DUE, WHEN IT IS IN YOUR POWER TO DO IT.
(Proverbs 3:27, RSV)

Lord, what makes it so easy to wait until it's too late
to give our bouquets to the living?
Are we afraid to express our caring side?
Or embarrassed by the love we feel?
Are we too self-concerned to give much thought to others?
Whatever the reason, Lord, we'd like to change.
Help us find ways to express our love, our appreciation, our praise.
Then, when death separates us,
the flowers we send will be a final tribute,
not an apology;
and the tears we shed will be for what was,
not for what might have been. Amen.

THE LABORERS IN THE VINEYARD

In our story for today, we see that God's grace is generously given to all. (Matthew 20:1-6)

Early one morning a landowner went out to hire laborers. "I will pay one denarius for a day's work in my vineyard," he said. The laborers agreed to that amount and headed into the vineyard.

Later that day, the landowner saw other men standing idle in the marketplace. He walked over to them and said, "Go into the vineyard. I will pay you whatever is right." Still later, the landowner went out and offered work to more laborers.

That evening, the owner of the vineyard said to his steward, "Call the laborers and pay them. Begin with the last who went to work."

The men hired late in the day each received one denarius. This pleased the men who had been hired first. They thought they would surely receive more, because they had worked longer. But the steward handed each of them one denarius as well! The men looked at their pay and complained, "These last men hired worked only one hour, yet you pay them the same as those of us who worked all day in the hot sun!"

"I am doing you no wrong," the landowner replied. "Did you not agree to work for one denarius? Take what belongs to you, and go. I choose to give the same to everyone. May I not do what I choose with money that belongs to me? Or do you think I should not be generous?"

SHARE

Like so many other stories that Jesus told, this one has several ideas we could talk about. One is that of being dissatisfied. It's no secret that many of us are never really satisfied. Moms and dads are a bore and spoil all the fun. Teachers don't live up to our expectations. The pastor brings up subjects we don't want to hear about. The new mayor or governor is at least as bad as the old one. And so it goes, on and on. Instead of talking about our dissatisfactions, let's be positive. When are we most happy in our family? What changes could we make to improve the quality of our life together? (Be specific. Consider such things as bathroom schedules, noise, TV viewing habits, drinking, sarcasm.)

FOLLOW UP

Moms and dads, get a sitter for the kids and go away for a weekend.

Make a list of positive actions that would make life together more satisfying. Post it near the table where you eat family meals. Be sure to praise one another for trying to practice those actions.

Generosity need not be measured in dollars and cents. Go out of your way to perform one generous act this week.

I HAVE LEARNED, IN WHATEVER STATE I AM, TO BE CONTENT. (Philippians 4:11, RSV)

Lord, how quickly we become dissatisfied!
The perfectly good tennis shoes or jeans aren't right
because they're not the name brand that's in just now.
The trip we'd looked forward to was spoiled
because we soon tired of the long drive
and took our boredom out on one another.
The job we were once so grateful for is now beneath us.
Lord, how desperately we need your guidance!
Let us understand that contentment
doesn't come from outside ourselves but from within.
Help us rediscover the peace that comes from you alone.
We ask this in Jesus' name. Amen.

JESUS MEETS ZACCHAEUS

In our story for today, we see how one man restored his relationship with the Lord. (Luke 19:1-10)

Zacchaeus was the chief tax collector in Jericho and a very wealthy man. The people he collected taxes from were convinced that he'd gotten rich by cheating them.

One day Zacchaeus heard that Jesus would be passing through Jericho. Curious about this person, he joined the people who had gathered along the road leading into town.

Zacchaeus was a short man, and the taller people in front of him cut off his view. So he ran ahead and climbed up into a sycamore tree. There he sat on a low branch and waited for Jesus to pass by.

When Jesus came to the tree, he looked up and saw the tax collector. "Come down quickly, Zacchaeus," he said, "for I must stay at your house today."

How surprised Zacchaeus must have been! He hurried down from the tree and joyfully led Jesus to his home.

People in the crowd were disgusted and murmured, "Jesus has gone to be the guest of a sinner."

Zacchaeus surely knew how the people felt about him. As he stood before Jesus, he said, "Lord, I will give half my belongings to the poor right now. And if I have cheated anyone, I will pay the person back four times the amount."

Jesus replied, "Zacchaeus, today salvation has come to this house."

SHARE

Just as Jesus forgave Zacchaeus, God forgives us. No matter what we have done to separate ourselves from God, we can be reunited. But there is one requirement. We have to be willing to confess our sins and seek the forgiveness that is so freely offered to us. Let's talk about our church today. What opportunities does it offer us to seek forgiveness and be reconciled with God and with one another? Why do we, or don't we, take full advantage of these opportunities?

FOLLOW UP

Children find it difficult, if not impossible, to relate to a *loving* God if they don't experience love at home. Love your children and assure them that you *like* them, too. Make it clear that you love them even when they do wrong—that it is the wrong action you dislike, not them.

Discuss how the concept of sin may change as you grow older.

Seek reconciliation with the Lord this week.

IF WE CONFESS OUR SINS, HE IS FAITHFUL AND JUST, AND WILL FORGIVE. (1 John 1:9, RSV)

You never turn away from us, Lord,
but sometimes we turn away from you.
During these few remaining days of Lent,
we want to change;
but we are weak and need your help.
Lord, be a mirror that lets us see ourselves
not only as we really are
but also as we might become.
Fill us with the will to repent.
Then grant us the peace that comes
from being reunited with you. Amen.

THE LAST JUDGMENT

One day we will be judged on the way we have lived our lives. In our story for today, we learn that judgment will be based on the way we have treated one another. (Matthew 25:31-40)

When the final judgment comes, the Lord will gather the people of all nations before him. The Lord will divide people into two groups, much the way a shepherd separates sheep from goats. Some will go to the right and some to the left. To those on his right the Lord will say, "Come, you who are blessed. Come and inherit the kingdom that has been prepared for you. For I was hungry and you gave me food; I was thirsty and you gave me drink; I was a stranger and you welcomed me; I was naked and you clothed me; I was sick and you took care of me; I was in prison and you visited me."

Those who are chosen will be puzzled. They will say, "Lord, when did we see you hungry and feed you, or thirsty and give you drink? When did we see you a stranger and welcome you, or naked and clothe you? And when did we see you sick and care for you? When did we visit you in prison?"

The Lord will answer them saying, "Whenever you acted with kindness to one of the least of my brothers and sisters you did so to me."

SHARE

Life has a rhythm. Day turns to night, and seasons turn one into another. Our lives, too, have a rhythm. We are born, we grow, we die. As Christians, we believe that the rhythm does not stop with death, but that it continues as we go on to new life in the presence of God. But before that occurs there is to be a final judgment. Let's consider what that judgment might be like, remembering that God is a God of love. As our Creator, how would a loving God expect us to have used our gifts of body? Mind? Spirit?

FOLLOW UP

Take time alone to consider your spiritual condition. If you knew you were to die in an accident tomorrow, what would you do today?

Begin a journal in which you record your spiritual development.

Make up a family prayer which stresses God's loving concern for us. Say the prayer each day this week so that everyone begins to appreciate that life is a gift to be used wisely.

LET THE WORDS OF MY MOUTH, AND THE MEDITATION OF MY HEART, BE ACCEPTABLE IN THY SIGHT. (Psalm 19:14, KJV)

Lord, we pray that when our life is ended
and the time for judgment comes,
you will find us worthy to live with you
forever.
Until that time,
help each of us be a candle
that lights the way for others. Amen.

THE WIDOW'S OFFERING

In our story for today, we hear a message about giving. (Mark 12:41-44; Luke 21:1-4)

There were offering boxes just outside the main part of the Temple. On a particular day, Jesus sat nearby, watching the people come and go. Many of the rich came to the boxes and put in large sums. Then Jesus noticed a poor widow come to make her offering. She dropped in only two copper coins. Together they were worth about a penny.

Upon seeing this, Jesus called his disciples to him. "This poor widow put more in the offering box than all the others," he said. "The rich put in what they had to spare. But poor as the widow is, she put in all that she had."

SHARE

Giving until it hurts is not a popular idea. Most of us find it difficult, if not impossible, to give the way the widow did in today's story. During times of inflation, families feel even more pressure to take care of themselves before thinking of anyone else's needs. As we enter the closing days of Lent, let's consider our attitudes toward sacrifice. What do we think of tithing (giving a per cent of our income)? What is our attitude toward giving up something for Lent? When is giving up something a good thing for the individual but perhaps not so good for others? (Consider how dieting and quitting smoking during Lent could be selfish actions.) In what ways do we give of our time? Our talents?

FOLLOW UP

Review your contributions to church and charity and make any changes you consider appropriate.

Teach older children how to budget to help them understand how costly it is to run both a family and a church.

Join with others to form a group whose purpose is to resolve some school, church, or neighborhood problem.

EVERYONE MUST GIVE ACCORDING TO WHAT HE HAS INWARDLY DECIDED; NOT SADLY, NOT GRUDGINGLY. . . . (2 Corinthians 9:7, NAB)

Lord, we see our own needs so much more clearly
than we see the needs of others.
Yet within us there is this urge
to be a cheerful giver,
for we know that through giving
we also receive.
Help us to put aside narrowness and stinginess.
Show us how to give more freely. Amen.

STRAINING FORWARD TO WHAT LIES AHEAD, I PRESS ON TOWARD THE GOAL. (Philippians 3:13-14, RSV)

GATHER

Gather the family around a table or wherever you can all be comfortable and have eye contact with one another. Be close enough so that you can easily join hands while praying. Choose a leader and two readers.

LIGHT A CANDLE

Light a candle as a sign to everyone that the time you spend together has special significance—you are placing yourselves in the presence of the Lord.

SING

Sing "This Little Light of Mine" on page 11 or another song of your choice that is appropriate for Palm Sunday.

PRAY

Leader: Let's join hands as we turn to God in prayer.

Lord, on this Palm Sunday, we prepare to celebrate Holy Week. In these final days before Easter, give us the insight we need to recognize our own faults and the strength to overcome them. Amen.

READ SCRIPTURE

First Reader: Today we're going to read about Jesus' entry into Jerusalem. Jesus had come to Jerusalem many times before, but this day was different. By now, word had spread about the amazing things he had said and done. People gathered along the roadway leading into the city to catch a glimpse of Jesus and to shout his praises. Here is what Mark says about it in his Gospel:

> [Jesus] sent off two of his disciples with the instruction: "Go to the village straight ahead of you, and as soon as you enter it you will find tethered there a colt on which no one has ridden. Untie it and bring it back. If anyone says to you, 'Why are you doing that?' say, 'The Master needs it but he will send it back here at once.'" So they went off, and finding a colt tethered out on the street near a gate, they untied it. Some of the bystanders said to them, "What do you mean by untying that colt?" They answered as Jesus had

told them to, and the men let them take it. They brought the colt to Jesus and threw their cloaks across its back, and he sat on it. Many people spread their cloaks on the road, while others spread reeds which they had cut in the fields. Those preceding him as well as those who followed cried out: "Hosanna! Blessed is he who comes in the name of the Lord!...Hosanna in the highest!"

Mark 11:1-10, NAB

SHARE AND REFLECT

Second Reader: There were great expectations among the people of Jerusalem. Of course we know that dark times were soon to follow. But for the moment there surely was tremendous hope as the people cried, "Hosanna! Hosanna!" The word means "come and deliver" and that is what the people expected Jesus to do. They expected him to come into their lives and set them free. As we relive our Christian history on this Palm Sunday, we too have great expectations. Although this is the week when we remember Jesus' death, we will also remember that he was victorious over death. Today we are going to talk about the "Victory of Love" and how it applies to our lives.

When are some of the times that our family has had great expectations? (Consider the birth of a child, moving, changing jobs, marrying, planning a vacation.)

What happens when we have great expectations and they don't work out the way we had hoped? How do we resolve dashed hopes? What role does love play then?

What is our image of God? Do we think primarily of someone who loves? Someone who punishes? Someone who will deliver us? Do we have other images of God?

CLOSE WITH A PRAYER

Leader: Dear Lord, we know that, like Jesus, we experience moments of triumph. But every life also includes some dark days. Then it is easy to lose hope. When we feel darkness or pain, help us remember that your love is always with us. As we make our journey through life, strengthen us to carry our own burdens and to share those of others. Amen.

FOLLOW UP

Extend your family time together by doing one or more of the following activities.

Look through old newspapers and magazines for stories about people who have overcome great difficulties. Do the stories in any way reflect the "victory of love"? If so, how?

Take the whole family for a walk. Go somewhere where you can relax and be open to the wonders of this world God created.

Discuss what Holy Week services you will be able to attend as a family. Is there someone outside your family who might like to go but has no transportation? Call and offer a ride.

TREATS

Have a treat such as popcorn at home, or take everyone out for ice cream.

THE MONEY-CHANGERS IN THE TEMPLE

The Temple in Jerusalem was the holiest of places. In our story for today, we learn that we are to respect houses of worship. (Mark 11:15-17; Matthew 21:-12-13; Luke 19:45-48; John 2:13-22)

After Jesus had made his triumphal entry into Jerusalem, he went to the Temple. There he found bankers exchanging foreign monies. They were charging a very high commission. He also found people selling pigeons to pilgrims as sacrificial offerings. The prices they were charging were much too high.

It angered Jesus to see people cheating others in this holy place. He overturned the tables of the money-changers. He tipped the stools of those who sold pigeons. Coins spilled and pigeons flapped about as Jesus drove the bankers and merchants out.

Jesus then turned to the people and told them, "In Scripture it is written that God said, 'My temple will be called a house of prayer for all people.' But you have turned it into a den of thieves."

SHARE

As Christians, we have an obligation to live up to our beliefs. At times we are likely to be morally outraged, as Jesus obviously was when he found the money-changers in the Temple. By his actions Jesus let us know that there are times when we are obliged to be angry at wrongdoing and injustice. Let's talk about our own feelings of being morally outraged by the behavior of others. Maybe it's corruption in government, injustice where we work, discrimination in the community. What feelings do situations such as these call forth in us? How do we deal with them? What can we do to turn our anger into a constructive force?

FOLLOW UP

Either draw pictures or make a list of words which show how you feel when you're angry.

Make it a habit to tell others how you are feeling.

As an outlet for personal anger, write letters about your feelings and then destroy them. Or write well-reasoned letters to the editor and send them in.

LET NOT THE SUN GO DOWN UPON YOUR WRATH.
(Ephesians 4:26, KJV)

Lord, help us express our sense of moral indignation
in purposeful ways.
When schools don't do their job,
let us find new ways to teach our children.
When one family member abuses another,
let us seek help instead of acting helpless.
When another country is ripped by war,
let us send bread instead of bullets.
We ask, Lord, that you help us find ways to build
rather than to destroy. Amen.

THE GREATEST COMMANDMENTS

In our story for today, Jesus tells us which commandments are most important. (Mark 12:28-34; Matthew 22:34-40; Luke 10:25-28)

People often asked Jesus questions in an effort to trap him. One day after he had been asked three tricky questions in a row, he was asked one that seemed sincere. A teacher of the law came to him and said, "Of all the commandments, which is the greatest?"

Jesus had an immediate answer. "The most important commandment is this," he said: "Love the Lord your God with all your heart, with all your soul, with all your mind, and with all your strength."

Then Jesus went on to say, "The second most important commandment is this: You must love your neighbor as you love yourself. There is no other commandment more important than these two."

SHARE

Within each of us something very good is waiting to be released. That something is love, and God put it there. Once we discover the love within us, we're called to put it into action. How we do it is for us to decide. Let's share what we understand about love. What is romantic love? Parental love? Christian love? How are they alike? How do they differ? What place does love have in our family's life?

FOLLOW UP

Pray for someone you find difficult to love.

Give hugs all around. Be sure to say that you like as well as love one another.

Read Charlotte Zolotow's *The Quarreling Book* (Harper & Row).

Perform a loving action. For example, invite someone over for coffee, share baked goods, write a letter, vacuum the car.

PUT ON LOVE, WHICH BINDS EVERYTHING TOGETHER IN PERFECT HARMONY. *(Colossians 3:14, RSV)*

Lord, your son Jesus shows us that love always wins.
It is a force like no other.
Love sends women such as Mother Teresa
to comfort the sick and dying.
Love sees with clear eyes
that there is work to do
and then does it.
Lord, as we look around at the world we know,
help us put aside our feeling of insignificance
and realize that your love is waiting
to go to work through us. Amen.

WHO IS THE GREATEST?

In our story for today, we learn what we must do to enter the Kingdom of God. (Matthew 18:1-4; Mark 9:33-37; Luke 9:46-48)

The disciples quarreled among themselves about who was most favored by Jesus. They were probably wondering who would have a position of power in the Kingdom that was to come. There was never any way for them to be sure who had the answer. So one day the disciples went right to Jesus and asked, "Who is of the greatest importance in the kingdom of God?"

Jesus did not answer their question directly. Instead, he called a little child over and stood him in front of the disciples. "Unless you change and become like little children, you will not enter the kingdom of God," Jesus told them. "The greatest in the kingdom are those who humble themselves and become like this child."

SHARE

Jesus' disciples were concerned about power and position. Like them, we are often worried about our position in life; about who we have power over and who has power over us. From our earliest years, we establish ourselves in positions of power. We run races to see who is the fastest; wrestle to see who is strongest; take tests to see who is the smartest. The recognition of power stays with us throughout life. People who work in sales are constantly reminded of their position relative to others in their organization. In sports we talk about power plays and power hitters. Let's talk about how *we* are affected by power. What power do we have? When do we feel the urge to lord it over others? How do we feel when others flaunt their power? When Christians attain positions of power, how should they live?

FOLLOW UP

If your family operates under the power principle where someone always acts as the boss, consider how your life would change if you lived more cooperatively. Involve everyone in making family rules.

Share your own power by teaching someone a skill you have.

REFLECT UPON WHAT HAS BEEN ASSIGNED TO YOU.
(Sirach 3:22, RSV)

Lord, we sometimes daydream about all the things we would do
if we were in a position of power.
Instead of daydreaming about what might be,
encourage us to make the best of what is.
Help us appreciate that we are an interdependent people.
We need janitors as well as journalists,
programmers as well as presidents,
farmers as well as financiers.
Then let us recognize the power within each of us—
the power to be honest and kind;
the power to say yes to you, Lord.
Keep us ever aware of our own power
and grant us the will to use it wisely. Amen.

THE LAST SUPPER

It was the custom of Jesus and his disciples to share the Passover meal that marked the Israelites' passage from slavery to freedom. In our story for today, we learn about the beginning of the Eucharist in a Passover setting. (Mark 14:12-16, 22-25; Matthew 26:17-19, 26-30; Luke 22:7-20)

The disciples came to Jesus and said, "Where do you want us to go to make preparations for the Passover meal?"

"Go into Jerusalem," Jesus told them. "There a man carrying a pitcher of water will meet you. Follow him, and go into the house that he enters. Say to the owner of the house, 'The Master wants to know where the dining room is in which he and his disciples can eat the Passover meal.' The owner will show you a large upper room that is furnished and ready for us."

The disciples set out and found everything just as Jesus had told them. They then went about preparing the meal.

When everything was prepared, Jesus and the disciples came to the table. Jesus took some bread. Saying the blessing, he broke the bread and gave it to his disciples. "Take it and eat," he said. "This is my body." Then he took a cup of wine. When he had given thanks, he gave the cup to his disciples. All drank from it, and he said to them, "This is my blood which is to be poured out for many."

SHARE

On this day we are reminded that Jesus acts on our behalf. We cannot completely understand all that he did and does for us, but we can reflect on his loving actions. He listens. He serves. He calms. He heals. He invites us to come to Communion. The spiritual food which he offers links us to all members of the Christian community. We have roots that go back to the moment at the Last Supper when Jesus shared himself with his friends. The pain of Good Friday is close at hand, and still we have every reason to be hopeful. Let's be silent for a moment and think how important hope is to us. (Pause.) What hopes do we have in our family? (Consider both family and individual hopes.) How do we help one another to make our hopes come true? What role does faith have in our hopes?

FOLLOW UP

Take part in the Holy Eucharist as a family.

Read John 13:1-17. Then wash and dry one another's feet.

Have a Passover meal. Serve roast lamb, matzos (unleavened bread), Passover salad (see the recipe on page 9), wine for grownups and grape juice for children. For dessert, serve a lamb-shaped cake. Bake it in a mold, or cut an oblong cake in the shape of a lamb. Ice it with coconut frosting and use it as a centerpiece with candles on either side.

*FEAR NOT, FOR I AM WITH YOU, BE NOT DISMAYED,
FOR I AM YOUR GOD; I WILL STRENGTHEN YOU, I
WILL HELP YOU. (Isaiah 41:10, RSV)*

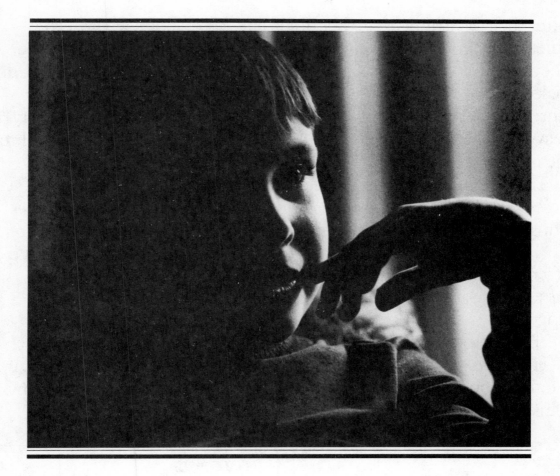

Lord, your promises give us hope.
As we stand in the shadow of Good Friday,
we are aware of ordinary things made extraordinary.
Simple bread and wine became a meal
to be remembered forever.
Each time we come to your table,
fill us with the hope that transforms lives.
We ask this in Jesus' name. Amen.

THE CRUCIFIXION

Jesus attracted such a large following that the rulers of the country considered him a threat. They feared that Jesus wanted their positions and their power. In our story for today, we see how the rulers dealt with this problem. (Luke 23; Matthew 27; Mark 15; John 18-19)

After their last supper together, Jesus and his disciples went to the quiet of a garden to pray. Roman soldiers soon interrupted them. They arrested Jesus and took him away to a place where he was put on trial. Then, even though Jesus had commited no crimes, he was sentenced to death—death on the cross. Soldiers forced Jesus to carry a heavy wooden cross to a place called Golgotha. There he was nailed to the cross and left to die.

Two criminals had also been crucified that day. Jesus hung on a cross between them. One of the criminals scoffed, "If you are the Christ, why don't you save yourself and us too?"

"Have you no fear of God at all?" the other criminal replied. "We deserved our sentence, but this man has done no wrong." Then he turned and said, "Jesus, remember me when you come into your kingdom."

"I will," Jesus promised. "Today you shall be with me in paradise."

From the sixth hour to the ninth, darkness came over the land. At the ninth hour Jesus cried out, "Father, into your hands I commit my spirit." With these words, Jesus died.

SHARE

We are mistaken if we think that because Jesus is the Son of God his suffering on the cross was less painful for him than it would be for us. Jesus was human as we are human and he accepted suffering as part of the human condition. His agony was real; he felt pain sharply; he knew the isolation of those who are depressed and feel abandoned. Jesus took on the aches of those who suffer from migraines, and he endured the battering known by the abused. Let's talk about our reaction to suffering and death. How well do we handle pain? How do we react to those who have long-term illnesses? What is our attitude toward people who live in nursing homes? Would we prefer to die at home, or in a hospital?

FOLLOW UP

Pray for those you know who are suffering.

Take a family discovery walk. Find examples of the life cycle as it is seen in nature so that you appreciate and remember the naturalness of change.

Attend Good Friday services at your church.

WE KNOW WE HAVE PASSED OUT OF DEATH INTO LIFE, BECAUSE WE LOVE. (1 John 3:14, RSV)

Lord, although this is a day of darkness,
help us sense the full meaning of Good Friday.
The day is *good* because Jesus endured
the pain and agony of the cross,
and did for each of us what we cannot do for ourselves.
Thank you, Lord, for your goodness and mercy. Amen.

JESUS IS LAID IN THE TOMB

In our story for today, we hear about the burial of Jesus. (Luke 23:50-56; Matthew 27:57-61; Mark 15:42-47; John 19:38-42)

For those who loved and followed Jesus, the hours after his death were a time of intense sadness. His followers must have felt that part of themselves had died along with Jesus. He still hung on the cross. Their beloved leader was dead. They felt sick at heart, and no one seemed to know what to do. Who would claim the body?

Then Joseph of Arimathea came forward. He was a wealthy and honorable man and a member of the council that had condemned Jesus to death. But he did not agree with what the council had done.

Joseph went to the ruler named Pilate and asked for Jesus' body. With Pilate's permission, he went to the cross and gently wrapped Jesus' body in a linen sheet. Then he took the body to his own tomb which had been dug out of rock. Joseph placed Jesus inside the tomb and then rolled a huge stone across the entrance. He had done all he could do.

SHARE

Christian hope has its roots in the three days spanning Jesus' death and resurrection. When Jesus was crucified, the darkness that came upon the world darkened people's spirits as well. They felt that the promises they had wanted so much to believe in had, in Jesus' death, come to a sad and brutal end. They did not yet know that on the third day Jesus would rise from the dead and fulfill the promise of new life. Often in our own lives we let hope die too easily. We can learn from the death-resurrection experience to apply a "three-day principle." When depressed, give sadness three days to die. When hurt, give feelings three days to heal. Let's think about our family. When have we acted too quickly? What are some situations we are involved in now to which we should apply the three-day principle?

FOLLOW UP

As a family, attend the Holy Saturday services your church conducts.

Prepare Easter-morning surprises for one another. (For young children the surprise might be hidden Easter baskets; for older ones, a small gift; for the whole family, a special breakfast of favorite foods.)

Read *Beyond Sorrow, Reflections on Death and Grief* by Herb & Mary Montgomery (Winston Press). Keep a copy on hand to give to someone who is grieving over the death of a loved one.

BE STRONG AND OF GOOD COURAGE....
(Joshua 1:9, RSV)

Lord, sometimes we feel depressed
and see only the negative side of life.
Death is especially hard to comprehend,
hard to accept.
Help us see that it is as natural to die
as to be born.
When we feel sorrow, help us understand
that our grief is a sign that we have loved.
Lord, we thank you for Jesus who overcame death
and gave us the promise of everlasting life. Amen.

THIS IS THE DAY WHICH THE LORD HAS MADE; LET US REJOICE AND BE GLAD IN IT. (Psalm 118:24, RSV)

GATHER

(In anticipation of a busy day and family church attendance, the suggested devotions for Easter Sunday are quite short.) Gather the family around a table or wherever you can all be comfortable and have eye contact with one another. Be close enough so that you can easily join hands while praying. Choose a leader and two readers.

LIGHT A CANDLE

Light a candle as a sign to everyone that the time you spend together has special significance—you are placing yourselves in the presence of the Lord.

PRAY

Leader: Let's join hands as we turn our hearts to God in prayer.

Thank you, Lord, for being near us during our lenten journey of love. Now Lent is ended. Easter is here! Let us rejoice and be glad. Amen.

READ SCRIPTURE

First Reader: It was near dawn of the first day of the week. Mary Magdalene and another woman who was also named Mary went to the tomb where they believed Jesus had been placed. When they got there, they saw an angel. Matthew tells us what happened then:

> The angel said to the women, "Do not be afraid; for I know that you seek Jesus who was crucified. He is not here; for he has risen, as he said."

Matthew 28:1-6, RSV

CLOSE WITH A PRAYER

Second Reader: The promise is fulfilled. Christ has died. Christ is risen. Christ will come again. The resurrection has taken the sting out of suffering, and death is not the end. There is more to come. There is new life for all who believe. Amen.

SING

Sing "Jesus Christ Is Risen Today" on page 10 or another appropriate Easter hymn.

FOLLOW UP

If you are eating dinner at home today, place your decorated Easter candle at the center of your table. Light it before saying grace and leave it burning through the meal.

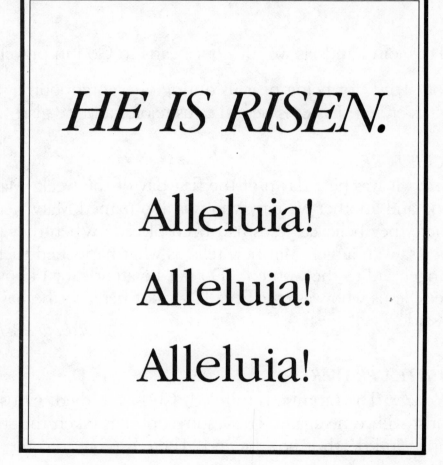

HE IS RISEN.

Alleluia!

Alleluia!

Alleluia!